6-15-73

Land of Hidden Fires
Løynde eldars land

Land of Hidden Fires
Løynde eldars land

by Tarjei Vesaas

**Translated, with an introduction
by FRITZ KÖNIG *and Jerry Crisp***

University of Northern Iowa

Wayne State University Press   Detroit, 1973

Title of original edition: *Løynde eldars land.*
Copyright © 1953 by Gyldendal Norsk Forlag, Oslo.

Norwegian text of the poems reproduced by permission of Gyldendal
Norsk Forlag and of Halldis Moren Vesaas.

Published simultaneously in Canada
by the Copp Clark Publishing Company
517 Wellington Street, West
Toronto 2B, Canada.

Library of Congress Cataloging in Publication Data

Vesaas, Tarjei, 1897–1970.
    Land of hidden fires.

    Poems.
    Bibliography: p.
    I. König, Fritz, 1940–   tr.
II. Crisp, Jerry, tr. III. Title.
PT9088.V6L6 1973   839.8′2′172   72-11951
ISBN 0-8143-1496-1

Contents 1754308

Acknowledgments

Above all I would like to extend my sincerest thanks to my co-translator, Jerry Crisp, who has devoted long hours of discussion and quiet work to give many of the English versions the necessary poetic essence; his expertise helped shape the poems in their final form. I am deeply indebted to Mrs. Halldis Moren Vesaas, Tarjei Vesaas's widow, in her own right a poet, who read the manuscript, gave many invaluable suggestions, and supported the project in every way she could. Her encouragement meant very much, not only in relation to this book. My thanks go to my old friend Kjetil Flatin, University of Chicago, who also subjected the manuscript to a critical reading and to John M. Lyon, Davis, California, a former student of mine, who assisted me with my first Vesaas translations. Gyldendal Norsk Forlag, the Norwegian publishing house of the original, has to be commended for its cooperation; and last but not least I am beholden to my wife for her careful and critical comparison of the English versions with the original and for her typing services.

Fritz König
Cedar Falls, Iowa, March 1972.

Introduction
Language and literature in Norway briefly considered

I remember first reading Sigrid Undset's famous trilogy *Kristin Lavransdatter* in German translation. I was a 21-year-old student who had never been to Norway. Four years later I reread the books after having lived in Norway for a time, and suddenly the story teemed with life; I could actually see the mountains and valleys come alive. I understood the significance of words like *winter* and *summer,* words which have far different connotations for someone used to mild winters and long summers; and the thoughts and feelings expressed by Undset's *dramatis personae* became strangely familiar. Thus, I think it is in order to preface a collection of Norwegian poetry translated for the non-Scandinavian public with a few words about Norway and her people. The reader should of course keep in mind that the following remarks are quite general and not without pitfalls.

Norway's unique identity seems to be formed by several different elements, all of which are somehow interlaced. First and most important is undoubtedly the overwhelming, dramatic landscape, rich with contrasts. Vast forests merge with softly undulating farmland, steep mountains drop into a clear, blue sea; in the north the primeval tundra; in the south, the sunny beaches and arable plains. In the middle of the last century Ivar Aasen described it well in his poem "Old Norway":

> Old Norway, northernmost in the world,
> she is our forefathers'.
> There is the ocean which from end to end

plays around the long beach.
There are bays and lakes and islands,
a thousand fjords and a thousand mountains,
snow covered plains, where the snow never melts
valleys with majestic waterfalls.

Despite the long winter
our pine forest still stands green
and when the leaves sprout forth on the slopes
our landscape is clad in beauty.
Long days, short nights
span lightly around the shining earth.
Beach and fjord and mountain and farmstead
reflect the sun from south and north . . . .[1]

Here are all the aspects that compose nature in Norway:
ocean, beaches, islands, mountains, lakes, waterfalls; they
are all there, as well as the different seasons in their northern
extremes: the everlasting dark winter and the short hectic
summer with its midnight sun in the north. Aasen follows
these stanzas with an image of the people seen here as
the typical Norwegian farmer still living on the lands tilled
by his forefathers hundreds of years ago. Most important
of all, however, this poem speaks of the Norwegian's intense
love for this country, a love undiminished through the years.
Poems in the same vein as "Old Norway" have been written
throughout the one hundred years that separate us from
Aasen. Bjørnstjerne Bjørnson's poem: "Yes we love this
country / as it emerges / furrowed and weathertorn from
the waves . . . ," famous today as the Norwegian national
anthem, is only one example, perhaps the noblest of all.
But most poignantly, after World War II, a love for Norway
finds expression, as in "Norwegian Love Song," by Tor
Jonsson:

I am the pine tree, dark and fierce.
You are the birch tree. You are bride
standing under peaceful sky—
we are both Norwegian nature.

I am soil, deep and black.
You are seed grain, clean and shining.
You are bearer of all our hopes.
We are both what we became.

I am mountain and naked slope.
You are lake and in it sky.
Both are we the land.
You are mine forever.

The creation of similar poetry in the other western countries after World War II is almost unthinkable; if it existed it would surely be unreadable. Strangely enough, in the Norwegian atmosphere such a poem sounds genuine and heartfelt and means exactly what it says. Thus we have to understand that nature is one of the thematic backbones in Norwegian literature, starting with the baroque poet Petter Dass's description of northern Norway down to the poetry of Tarjei Vesaas, for one. And for centuries this nature shaped the people. They are a hardy race, seasoned by the age-old fight for survival.

Nature has always been a mixed blessing for the Norwegians. The land has yielded little and the ocean has not given up its riches without a struggle. In early times when the rest of Europe toiled under the yoke of feudalism, the Norwegian farmer enjoyed relative freedom on an isolated farm, separated from neighboring farms by a steep mountain or a deep valley. This isolation made it difficult to assemble forces for national defense, but at the same time slowed down would-be invaders. In the nineteenth century this beautiful but forbidding and inhospitable nature forced the growing population into a mass exodus to America. It has been estimated that nearly as many people of Norwegian descent are to be found in the U.S. today as in Norway—with just under four million inhabitants. Moreover, the Norwegian climate and terrain in combination with a widely scattered population, did not invite industrialization in the nineteenth century. Today, lack of heavy industry is perhaps an asset since the ecological problems in Norway are minimal compared to those in more industrialized nations.

Just as the Norwegian landscape is a combination of dramatic contrasts, Norwegians themselves are complex and sometimes enigmatic. Norwegians (whose national legislature awards the coveted Nobel Peace Prize) love to engage in heated debates on international peace and how to best preserve it—yet sometimes shrug their shoulders when far simpler internal problems are discussed. Becoming militant over racial strife in the United States or South Africa (and even electing a black South African as president of the student body at Oslo University), they are sensitive when one mentions the low life expectancy and poverty of the nomadic Lapps in northern Norway. Such peculiar inconsistencies have prompted even young Norwegian poets to self-criticism of the national temperament, as for instance Kate Næss in "Norwegians":

> In winter they eat much blood
> In summer they're almost radicals
> The dairy woman sure enough
> thinks the town's new ambulance
> makes too much noise
> There has to be a limit to saving lives
> she says

Yet, Norwegians are, at the same time, a generous people.

They learned long ago to depend on and help their neighbors in the forbidding northern climate, and it comes as no surprise therefore that they have a highly advanced welfare system today. And whenever an international catastrophe occurs, like a flood or earthquake, they quickly contribute a surprising amount of *kroner* to help.

There are few urban areas in Norway—just five or six major ones. City life seems to go against the grain of many individualistic, nature-loving Norwegians; they try to escape from it as often as they can. On any given weekend with bearable weather, Oslo has a tendency to resemble Paris in August—deserted by the natives. Even in poems where the city is praised, something dark and untangible looms in the background, as in "Night in Oslo" by Tore Ørjasæter:

Oslo, Oslo resounds heavily
the melody of your old name.
Oslo, Oslo, Norway's heart,
the country's lifeblood pulses
through thoughts pregnant with feeling,
thoughts born in your embrace.
Look, from the fjord bright flashes
shine through the blackened night
marking the shipping lane into Oslo harbor.

Here I walk poor and lonely
in the cold night and tremble.
Oslo-town lies and dreams—
saga-heavy, just as I think—
only stars blink full of life
above me on the pale arch of heaven.
Deafened with the thunder of waterfalls
time flows steadily towards eternity
quietly like the whispering Akerselv.

Knut Hamsun's novel *Hunger* opens with the ominous lines: "There was a time when I walked around Kristiania [Oslo was so named until 1925], this strange town which no one leaves without having been marked by it. . . . " City life in Norway is different from that of other European cities. Norwegians are open-minded cosmopolitans—citizens of a nation that lives largely off its commercial fleet have to be. Most younger Norwegians speak a foreign language with some fluency. Nevertheless, there is no cosmopolitan atmosphere in Oslo or other major cities in Norway comparable to that of a city like Geneva. Geneva's elegant urbanity contrasts with a certain type of pioneering spirit found in Norway (not unlike the frontier spirit in northern Canada or Siberia) that is manifest in Norwegian interest in shipping and activity in the country's Arctic and Antarctic possessions. Moreover, the cities, however large they may be, always seem overshadowed by the surrounding rural areas, with a resulting strange blend of cosmopolitanism and provincialism.

While in both Ørjasæter's poem and Hamsun's lines we can detect a positive element, today's outlook seems generally more negative, as in J. M. Bruheim's poem "Crossroads":

> . . . I know no one—
>
> Still I long to call
> one, the one.
> Ask him to come.
> When I turn, I only hear
> the bare walls shout: you are alone.
>
> The traffic light blinks red and green.
> People like sleep walkers
> follow an invisible track—
> No one has time.

All have dead masks
no one speaks.

No one hears and no one sees.
They are led by a blind pilot.

A child walks against the light
and no one holds his hand.
He drowns—goes under—
he cannot save himself
cannot cannot—
can.

The feeling of being lost and unable to communicate is
strong here, despite the somewhat optimistic ending. But
perhaps the complexity of Norway as a country and a people
has been captured best by Marie Takvam in her poem
"Norway":

In bread and cod liver oil lies our most sacred sacra-
        ment.
We are closer to Greenland than to Jerusalem
now and forever.
Norwegian exhibition of kinetic art:
Flaming tongues of northern lights
over enormous darkroom-vaults
glittering hallucinations
incomprehensibly psychedelic
dying abruptly
and man sees small pinhead-diamonds
freezing on the blue stretched silk
over the suburbs' Nirvana:
marriages compressed by concrete.

Cranes lift iron beams, pipes
long straws in their pelican-bills, hard nests.
People come from fjords and mountains—
clot together slip into eighty square yards
are pressed into blocks as well as
can be expected with such material.

After its stunning beauty, the second element which helps
to explain modern Norwegian civilization is simply the
imprint of its long history on its people. From a little known
past, Norway erupted like a volcano during the Middle
Ages. Norwegian Vikings harried the coasts of Europe,
settling in France (Normandy) and the islands in the Atlantic,
Great Britain, Ireland, the Shetlands, Orkneys, Hebrides,
Faeroes, Iceland, and Greenland. In the tenth century people
left for Iceland on the same scale as they left roughly a
thousand years later for America, except that reasons for
the earlier emigration were political rather than economic.
The free Norwegian farmer left home to avoid paying taxes
to a king (Harald Fairhair unified Norway in the ninth
century). While the tenth-century settlements in France,
Great Britain, and the surrounding islands soon merged
with the already existing culture, some of the northernmost
islands maintain their decisive Scandinavian character to
this day (the Faeroes and Greenland still belong to Denmark). Probably the most significant and lasting settlement
was the one in Iceland. The enterprising farmers who came
to Iceland kept their cultural and linguistic heritage intact
for a long time, as many colonial countries tend to do.
They were converted to Christianity later than were other
Scandinavians. Modern Icelandic is very close to Old Norse
and did not undergo one fourth of the linguistic changes
that influenced the other Scandinavian languages. But most
important here is that the new nation in Iceland created
a unique literature. Without many traceable traditions a
sudden literary golden age emerged of which a good deal

has been preserved and handed down to us: the lays of the Edda, the different types of sagas and many skaldic poems.

While cultural life and literature flourished in Iceland, Norway also flourished politically and economically. The Vikings brought not only immense riches back from Europe's shores but also influences which served partly to fertilize and partly to destroy their own culture. In the long run, Norway could not afford this loss of blood to Iceland. The Norwegian "Golden Age" was shortlived. Torn by inner strife, Norway was within a few decades on the decline. In 1349 the plague decimated its population. Eventually losing its sovereignty to Denmark, Norway was for over four centuries no more than a distant Danish province. The Danish administration brought its own language to Norway, and within two hundred years Norway had lost not only its autonomy but also its national language, which survived only in local dialects. The *lingua franca* was Danish. Norwegian literature from that period is virtually nonexistent.

After the French Revolution, a new political wind blew across Europe, national pride was again kindled in Norway and from that moment on through the German occupation during World War II down to our times Norway has been very much under the star of nationalism—a benevolent and self-centered sort of nationalism, lacking any missionary zeal. Even Norwegians make fun of their national awareness when it is carried to the extreme. Norway shook off the Danish yoke in 1814 only to exchange it for a Swedish one for another 100 years. Yet, in the early nineteenth century a national renaissance, both political and spiritual, occurred, helped on its way by German and British romanticism. Reborn also was Norwegian literature. Wergeland and Welhaven wrote poetry with basically nationalistic undertones; Camilla Collett and Bjørnstjerne Bjørnson helped form the Norwegian novel—and Ivar Aasen created a new Norwegian language.

Toward the middle of the century when the Grimm brothers and their linguistic followers were active in Germany, similar endeavors were made in Norway. While the Germans already had a language and literature of their own, the Norwegians almost had to start anew. How much more important it was for them to write down their lore and folksongs. Like the Grimm brothers, Asbjørnsen and Moe collected fairy tales. Delving into the Norwegian national heritage made it more and more imperative that Norwegians rid themselves of the Danish language, a foreign element which was especially troublesome since it was omnipresent. There were two alternatives: either to adapt Danish orthography to the Norwegian pronunciation and to take on more Norwegian idioms, or to build a national Norwegian language from Old Norse and different Norwegian dialects, thus achieving artificially what the historical development denied. Both possibilities had their followers. During the second half of the nineteenth century written Danish began its transformation into a written Norwegian. Both Ibsen and Bjørnson still wrote Danish around the turn of the century, Hamsun even for some time after that. But after 1900 the trend toward written Norwegian accelerated, and roughly every one or two decades there has been a spelling reform, with the result that not many people in Norway spell alike. The product of these changes, called *riksmål* earlier, today called *bokmål*, represents the national language written more than spoken by roughly 75 percent of the population. The remaining 25 percent speak and write some form of "New Norwegian," called *landsmål* earlier, *nynorsk* today. This language is unique since it perhaps is the only one which has been virtually created by one man, Ivar Aasen, from elements of dialects in south-central Norway and from Old Norse—an incredible feat. Not unlike Lessing, who turned into an artist only after he felt compelled to prove his criticism on the contemporary theater to be valid by writing plays himself, Aasen felt the urge to prove that the new language he had created was ready to be a literary language. He wrote both prose and poetry, still fresh and appealing today.

Like nature, language is both a blessing and a curse in Norway. Practical difficulties are overwhelming. It is a burden for a small country to struggle with two official languages, especially two so closely related, more closely than are Czech and Russian or Spanish and Portuguese. Norwegian schoolchildren are forced to study a second Norwegian language, along with English, German, and French. Language is beyond doubt both culturally and politically a separating force.[2] But this dualism has more than negative effects—there are advantages. One could say that it fertilizes to some degree the literary activities in the country; the contemporary literature is for such a relatively small nation astoundingly rich and varied.

Usually, when Norwegians talk about their national literature, they regard it as one body without separating *bokmål* from *nynorsk* literature. A history of *nynorsk* literature has yet to be written. This seems at first surprising since there is a certain degree of conflict among supporters of the two languages. But in literary works of art, the language aspect seems outweighed by the work of art itself, which thus provides a common denominator. Of course, there are other unifying elements such as general literary periods, schools of thought and that vast expanse of imagery and atmosphere that is the essence of Norwegian literature. Disregarding now the distant medieval Golden Age, Norwegian literature is young, even younger than American literature. Perhaps this is one of the reasons that it exudes an uncomplicated freshness rarely seen in other European literatures. Elements of decadence and artificiality are almost completely lacking. Again, in this context, the *nynorsk* literature is especially intriguing. Despite the diversity of works through the decades and the different stylistic trends, it forms a closely knit body of literature. What makes it unique is that, in its century of life, it has undergone the development which, for other European literatures, occupied hundreds of years.

Within a few decades of its conception, *nynorsk* developed into a medium of great expressive power. It is no coincidence that today more Norwegian writers turn to *nynorsk* than would be expected from the proportion of Norwegians who speak it. Writers who come from areas of the country where *nynorsk* normally is not spoken use it as their literary medium. By now the already rich literary tradition includes Aasen, Vinje, Garborg, Duun, Ørjasæter, Nygard, and Vesaas as some of the milestones. Upon being asked why he chose to write *nynorsk* only, Vesaas answered laconically that it did not occur to him to use anything else. But then, Vesaas's native Telemark is the heartland of *nynorsk*.

The wealth of Norwegian literature is amazing, especially if we take into account that the Norwegian writer has traditionally led a difficult life at home. The book market in Norway has always been limited; hence royalties are slim. But the more serious handicap has been the confinement of a provincial society where authors and other artists—who in all countries are eccentrics in the eyes of their fellow human beings—have been looked upon with suspicion. The one who felt this most keenly was probably Norway's most famous son, Ibsen, a voluntary exile for over twenty years. And most modern Norwegian writers, too, escape to the South once in a while (Vesaas loved to travel).

All these elements: Norwegian nature, cultural customs and history, the language situation, the late arrival in a modern age, and the pioneering spirit, help to account for a special breed of writer. One historian of Norwegian literature puts it this way:

> Constructive devotion is the key characteristic of Norwegian writers. Art for art's sake is practically non-existent. Writers have a clear aim in mind, a definite purpose varying in detail from author to author and from one period to the next, but always describable

in the words in which Ibsen expressed what he considered to be his vocation when, in the early 1860's, he applied to the King for a grant: to bring the Norwegian people to think in a great way. In that sense Norwegian writers have been missionaries, and might well have subscribed to Bjørnson's dictum: 'The calling of the poet is that of the prophet.'[3]

Tarjei Vesaas, his life and work.

I have to be grateful. Fate has shown me mercy, has let me do what I wanted to do most.

TARJEI VESAAS

On the occasion of Vesaas's seventieth birthday in 1967, a collection of articles by persons acquainted with the author was published, entitled *Tarjei Vesaas.*[4] Each one illuminates some aspect of his personality and work; three were especially significant. Johan Borgen, probably the most famous Norwegian novelist today, and a contemporary of Vesaas, writes:

One should learn how to be silent. That seems so intelligent. Tarjei Vesaas knows how to do that. But does he ever know how to speak, yes, really to communicate! He doesn't seem to be less intelligent then . . . . At the same time he doesn't express himself in words of wisdom.[5]

And the Swedish writer Johannes Edfelt says about Vesaas's language:

Under your language is a hidden language: an intense and eloquent silence, which, if listened to in the right way has so much to tell us about life in its depth, about the motions of the soul under the outer layers. Your language is signs and symbols for this secret life of the soul which you yourself are able to grasp with your keen ears.[6]

Another Swede, Britt Tunander, writing of a personal meeting and interview with Vesaas, appropriately entitles her short essay: "No big words."[7] All three articles point to one of the most distinctive traits in Vesaas's character and its reflection in his works: under a surface of silence he unfolds ultimate eloquence which concentrates on central issues, magnifying them in an unending chain of ever-new, ever-familiar symbols. The autobiographical material which Vesaas provides the reader[8] is, not at all surprisingly, meager; his brief essay "About the Writer" is all the more valuable.[9]

Others, however, have tried to shed more light on Vesaas's life, so that current bibliographies include two biographies of the poet and several articles about him. The earlier biography, by Ragnvald Skrede,[10] written in 1947, does not include Vesaas's last twenty-five years. The second, published in the year of Vesaas's death, is a rather detailed monograph on the poet's life and work by Kenneth G. Chapman.[11] It is a valuable source for Vesaas's later years.

Vesaas was born in 1897 on the ancient Vesaas farmstead in Vinje district, Telemark, in south-central Norway. As the first-born of three sons, he had the privileged position of being *odelsgutt* in the family; that is, he was expected to take over the farm upon coming of age. According to Vesaas's own words, he felt this as a heavy burden in his youth since he seemed unable to give this predestined farming future his undivided attention, being interested much more in two rather unrelated items: books and guns. Fortunately, his parents and brothers were very understanding and did not discourage his early reading and writing. As far as his relationship with his mother and father are concerned probably Goethe's well known words: "Vom Vater hab' ich die Statur des Lebens ernstes Führen, vom Mütterchen die Frohnatur und Lust zu fabulieren" describe it perfectly. His mother was interested in music and literature, his father in his profession and horses. But the elder Vesaas liked to read too, and his son tells about one summer in his youth when father, son, and a farmhand competed in reciting parts of Ibsen's *Peer Gynt* during their work.

Vesaas admits to remembering his early youth but dimly; he recalls, among other events, the death of Norway's two literary giants, Ibsen in 1906 and Bjørnson in 1910 and his rude awakening in 1914 with the arrival of World War I. He found consolation in his reading, especially the prose fiction of Hamsun, Kipling, and Lagerlöf. The Norwegian trio of poets, Aukrust, Nygard, and Bull helped form his sense for poetry. Vesaas's formal education concluded in 1917 with a year at Lars Eskeland's *folkehøgskole* (a form of adult education pioneered by the Scandinavians). Here he read much Tagore. During a short military interlude, while he was stationed with the Royal Guards in Oslo 1918/19, he made his first contact with the urban atmosphere and the theater. After this experience, and an unhappy love affair, he began to write.

After he received the usual number of publishers' rejection slips, the breakthrough came in 1923 with the short novel *Children of Man (Menneskebonn);* the next year brought another novel *Huskuld the Herald (Sendemann Huskuld).* In both novels Vesaas creates a lyrical atmosphere, especially in his landscape descriptions, an aspect he refines in the years to come. His characterizations are romantic at heart. But the real weakness of these books is a symbolism that is often not really convincing and a certain overtone of sentimentality.

Early literary success, although still on a relatively small scale, probably formed Vesaas's life more than any other event. It made the decision for him that he was to become a writer; the travel grants that followed enabled him to get much-needed experience abroad. Being away from home made him appreciate what he had left behind and helped him decide to settle down in his native Vinje for good.

His marriage to the poet Halldis Moren in 1934 signaled that the course of his life was set. He made his permanent home at the farm Midtbø in Telemark.

In the meantime, other books appeared. *Grinde Farm* and *Evening at Grinde* (*Grindegard,* 1925 and *Grindekveld,* 1926). These books, little read today, are important only in the circle of motifs they contain, to which Vesaas seems always to return. Much change is evident in the novel *The Black Horses* (*Dei svarte hestane,* 1928). That a film version of the book exists (from the 1950s) is no coincidence. For the first time he gathers his narrative around a central image (the black horses), something he is to do often in his later works. His earlier sentimentality is almost completely lacking. In this novel he develops a dramatic style. If it were not for the symbolism and lengthy soliloquies, the elliptical sentences and laconic dialog would suggest the Icelandic family saga. But Vesaas's work is still romantic, and his drama sometimes turns into melodrama.

In 1929 Vesaas moved into another prose genre with his first collection of short stories, *The Bell in the Mound* (*Klokka i haugen*). Probably the best one of the short stories is "Signe Ton." Here Vesaas succeeds in something he was never able to do before, blending atmosphere, plot, characters, and style into a single entity. What he accomplished here, using the frame of the short story, he could not rival in his novels for some years to come. It took the one-thousand-page *Dyregodt* tetralogy to prove to Vesaas that the epic form, in which Knut Hamsun and Sigrid Undset excelled, did not suit him well. The first and probably the best novel in this series, *Father's Journey* (*Fars reise*), was published in 1930. It is written in a convincing, intense style, making use of realistic characterization techniques. *Sigrid Stall-*

brokk (1931) is stylistically much weaker. The third, *The Unknown Men (Dei ukjende mennene,* 1932), brings a course correction in the plot and in the author's *Weltanschauung,* reflecting the precarious political situation of Europe in the 1930s. While in Vesaas's earlier works the characters were led on the Norne's thread of divine fate, they now start acting on their own moral convictions and from a feeling of duty and human responsibility. The fourth part, *The Heart Listens to Its Native Music (Hjarta høyrer sine heimlandstoner)* comes much later, in 1938, and is even less in harmony with the earlier books than part three. Vesaas himself says that the fourth volume was written in the series-novel fashion of the time. And it was also written because the main figure Klas was not developed in a way which still satisfied his creator in 1938. In short, he seems here, under the influence of his recent marriage and a new home, to solve some of his personal problems—just as he does in the *The Great Cycle (Det store spelet,* 1934). This is the most autobiographical of all his books, except for *The Boat in the Evening.* The motifs here are similar to the ones used in the Grinde books and the Dyregodt novels: the life on a farm.

The Great Cycle was followed in 1935 by a second volume, *Women Call: Come Home (Kvinnar ropar heim),* which is in its theme reminiscent of these earlier works. Again, the second volume is much weaker than the first. Vesaas himself admits:

> In the second volume . . . the author fell victim to a certain fury of childbirths . . . it became too much of a good thing. Perhaps it happened because while working on the book one knew all the time the strangely exciting fact: in this moment our own first child is growing—. The book became lopsided because of that. [12]

However, *The Great Cycle* itself is one of the most central and most often read works of Vesaas. It provided a second breakthrough for him, now on a much larger scale, of course. It is the final work of his early years—his final attempt at the broad epic form. It is the final and crowning book in which the farm and farm life provide the basic themes. His descriptions of the rural setting are so vivid and impressive that they are matched only by the work of writers like Hamsun and Duun. The symbolism is much more refined and far less conventional than before. Vesaas proceeds here from such macrocosmic symbols as sun, moon, and stars to microcosmic ones like the rustling of leaves or a certain momentary light reflection. Of this book Vesaas says:

> During all these years I knew that I wanted to write a book about *the farm* and the youth who grew up there, about the situation of the adults, about the thousand things that make a farm. It *had* to be written once, by me, in the somewhat strange circumstances that had emerged in my private life, I, having gone from the farm which I should have taken over. To rid myself of something by writing it. And as a sort of explanation to my people at home.
>
> Now, it is not right to see in *The Great Cycle* a direct accounting of my own childhood. The characters don't fit, nor do the actions, not even the result for Per the main figure in the novel—but it is true, all the same. More true than the pure truth of a detailed report would be. Per Bufast gave up his resistance when the great relationship in his life became clear to him. The author did the same, but in a different way. When one starts looking, everything wants to be part of a larger entity, to merge. If one really wants to live, one has to belong to the cycle. [13]

Thematically connected with the second of the Bufast novels *(Women Call: Come Home)* is the novel *The Sandalwood (Sandeltreet,* 1933), which deals with a pregnant woman's fear and its impact on a family that tries to understand. In 1936 a second collection of short stories appeared, *The Clay and the Wheel (Leiret og hjulet).* In many ways these short stories seem to be a by-product of the Bufast books. Rural life is again the center of interest.

If World War I was a traumatic experience for Vesaas, a war which he, after all, observed from a distance, World War II, which he experienced in his own country, influenced his life and his writing even more powerfully. Although Vesaas was very productive during the war, only one of the four books he wrote was published; the others were hidden until after 1945. He now finally seems to have settled for the literary genre that suits him best: the short novel. The four "war" books were written in that form; they are of a consistently high literary quality. Vesaas proves to be a master in the creation and handling of the symbols and of a special condensed, yet highly eloquent style. The first book is *The Seed (Kimen,* 1940). Although a short novel, it has many of the structural elements of a short story: one climax and a limited number of *dramatis personae.* The pace is more dramatic than epic; even the three Aristotelian unities are observed. *The Great Cycle* had been written with all his senses wide awake, but this book is even more perceptive. The whole atmosphere cannot only be seen, but felt, smelled and tasted as well. Most striking are those parts in the book that show the savage animal in man.

The Bleaching Place (Bleikeplassen, 1946) was published after the war. Whereas *The Seed* demonstrates man's savagery, *The Bleaching Place* attempts to explain the reasons behind it, which lie to a certain extent in his mental isolation. The characterizations in *The Seed* were abstract; in *The Bleaching Place* they grow thoroughly unreal. The third novel, *The Tower (Tårnet,* 1948) presents basically the same theme: man's isolation and the danger of it.

The House in the Darkness (*Huset i mørkret*, 1945), Vesaas's reaction to the war, is, in its action, an allegory of the Norwegian resistance. Man's isolation and the impeding moral conflicts again stand in the foreground. The characters are even more abstract than in the previous three novels.

Vesaas made only a few excursions into playwriting; drama was a genre that did not suit him too well, although he had enormous success with his radio plays. In 1934, Vesaas wrote a play called *Ultimatum*, dealing with the political shadows on Europe's horizons at that time. It was not very well received. In 1947 he created a dramatic version of *The House in the Darkness* entitled *The Morning Wind* (*Morgonvinden*), which was much weaker than the original novel. The '40s also saw Vesaas belatedly flowering into a lyric poet.

His next novel, *The Signal* (*Signalet*), published in 1950, provides a Kafkaeske reading experience in an entirely surrealistic setting. With another collection of short stories, *The Winds* (*Vindane*, 1952), Vesaas moves back again into the realm of realism—into his special world of lyrical realism. The collection won him the 1952 Venice Triennale Prize for the best European prose work published during that year. The stories, for the first time since the Bufast novels, again manifest a firm belief in the eternal life-giving forces. *Sun* and *bread* are central symbols. His last collection of short stories, *A Beautiful Day (Ein vakker dag)*, appeared in 1959.

Spring Night (*Vårnatt*, 1954), a novel, is a clear step back from the extreme allegorical form of *The Signal* to a novel more on the level of *The Bleaching Place*. In this novel, which is not without structural flaws, Vesaas still seems to be hesitating about whether to prefer allegorical or symbolic treatment. In *The Birds* (*Fuglane*, 1957), he creates a world sparkling with action that often crystallizes into a systematic pattern of symbols. It is probably Vesaas's best novel, with *The Great Cycle* and *The Ice Palace* being close seconds. There is a complete and harmonic blending of structure, plot, themes, style, and the use of the symbol.

After *The Birds* the pendulum swings back. *The Fire* (*Brannen, 1961*) is, like *The Signal*, a surrealistic novel with a dreamlike atmosphere. The characters are again abstract, colorless. Vesaas himself has said about *The Fire* and his other allegorical novel, *The Signal:*

> So-called incomprehensible novels have to be written too, I think. A way ahead of us needs to be opened. It has been said that the novel is dying—I don't believe it. It is impossible to think that fantasy will dry up in young people. Rather, they must have the freedom to create, using *their* images, not the ones of the older generation. The old ones can be oldest as much as they like. If one writes a little outside of the known and familiar circle, one soon receives dangerous notes. It is worst that the writer himself does not feel that this is oddly written or unfamiliar. E.g., *I* hear that I sometimes write so that no one understands a word of it. I, the originator, cannot get that into my head. This is straight forward, I think, how strange people are! But the author always has the ideal reader in mind who follows everywhere.
>
> One should write as one thinks it is best any time; one cannot have guidelines. If one should write like a thousand other people think it should be, not much would become of our poetic works.
>
> There is one of my books, it's called *The Signal.* It stands like some problem child, but its creator is forever happy to have written this story. Another impossible book is *The Fire.* But it was just truth to the writer at the time it was written. The form chose itself. I don't think there is anything meaningless or mystic in this story about Jon—but I cannot tell the

contents here, or I would destroy it. The reader has to read without prejudices, then perhaps he can feel what the author wanted to say. It is not written to be understood in cold blood. There has to be a good deal of that which the reader only *feels* inside himself. The reader must have a cause to open his own secret rooms. He has to feel the vibrations—and that he can, to a much greater extent than he imagines, thank God. [14]

Three more novels appear in the sixties: *The Ice Palace* (*Is-slottet,* 1963), *The Bridges* (*Bruene,* 1966) and *The Boat in the Evening* (*Båten om kvelden,* 1968). The best one is probably *The Ice Palace,* which won the Nordic Council Prize for Literature in 1964. In all three novels he picks up again where he left off with *The Birds.* With the exception of the last one they are realistic and symbolic—the two elements in Vesaas's books undergo a parallel development. The style is lyrical, more so in the last two than in *The Ice Palace.* In *The Boat in the Evening* whole paragraphs are purely lyrical.

His last book, *The Boat in the Evening,* though in style and form very much akin to *The Ice Palace* and *The Bridges,* is not realistic. Two chapters, however, are autobiographical, the first such personal witness, since the Bufast novels and some of his poems. Curiously enough, these two biographical works provide the frame around Vesaas's literary work. The books written before the Bufast novels are today of interest only to the student of literary history. *The Boat in the Evening* is the last larger work. Vesaas died in 1970, recognized internationally as one of the key figures in Norwegian, Scandinavian—perhaps even European—contemporary literature.

It is impossible to label Vesaas. He leads beyond the realistic tradition in the Norwegian novel, but at the same time few of his books are purely surrealistic. The pendulum swings from neoromanticism in his early works and in some of his poetry to impressionism and expressionism; from allegorical to symbolic treatment of his material and back again. He has written in most literary genres—large epic, short novel, short story, play, and lyric poem. We could encounter just as many difficulties again, if we tried to classify him by the school of thought he belongs to, or by his *Weltanschauung*. Kresten Nordentoft sums it up in his article "The Themes":

> Existentialism or psychoanalysis? Humanism or Christianity or a pantheistic unifying religiosity?—If one asked Tarjei Vesaas he would incline his head, look at the floor, mull it over, then turn around on his chair and say thoughtfully: "I don't know—"[15]

In spite of the variety, the changes in form, the different topics, there are unifying elements in Vesaas's work. We can pick up each single volume he ever wrote and say without hesitation: this is Vesaas.

Vesaas's lyric poetry

> You looked for a flower
> and found a fruit.
> You looked for a spring
> and found a sea.
> You looked for a woman
> and found a soul—
> you feel frustrated.
>
> E. Södergran

The Springs (*Kjeldene*, 1946) is the title of Vesaas's first collection of poetry. It would be vain to speculate whether the title is a coincidence or not; *the springs* as a poetic image surely has a long tradition in the poetry of Western Europe. It also is an appropriate heading for one's first collection of poetry. And Vesaas surely must have experienced something very much akin to what the Södergran poem describes. After making his debut as a lyric poet rather late in life, at age 49, he suddenly must have discovered the joy of writing poetry because the first trickle of poems in *The Springs* expands virtually into a sea of poetry. Within the next decade there are four more collections to come: *The Game and the Lightning (Leiken og lynet,* 1947); *Wanderers' Happiness (Lykka for ferdesmenn,* 1949); *Land of Hidden Fires (Løynde eldars land,* 1953); *May Our Dream Stay New (Ver ny vår draum,* 1956) and later a fifth anthology: *Life by the River (Livet ved straumen,* published posthumously in 1971).

In many ways it is surprising that Vesaas did not write poetry earlier than 1946. As early as the 1930s his prose style evinced a lyrical quality. Yet it is probably best to let Vesaas himself speak about the beginning of his poetry writing:

I should also say something about the lyric poet who made his belated debut in 1946. The reason for it can be found many years earlier when I first met Halldis Moren. She gave me a collection of poems to read by the unhappy but ingenious Finland-Swedish poet Edith Södergran. There is no way in which I could explain the miraculous effect this reading had. Especially when taken into consideration the form that was used in those poems. The whole thing was a disgruntling experience and it aroused interest in trying one's hand at poetry—as all outstanding and genuine art inspires and puts one in a frame of mind to work. But nothing more came of it, as before, no poems now either. It remained hidden in a quiet place for

14 years. Then it re-emerged for an unknown reason and resulted in the first poetic attempt in *The Springs*. And it was more enjoyable to work with than anything else.

The rhymeless poems—they aroused a desire to try, in this form I thought I could say more of what I wanted to say. All the magnificent poems I had read and held dear throughout my adult life, they did not have *that* effect. This new form on the other hand—. By the way, to call it a new form is nonsense, it is as old as the oldest poetry we know. Perhaps an old form in a new way.

The question is how far to go. To throw torn-off words onto a sheet and then let them lie there wherever they settle down, I think is dubious poetry—but I think it's all right for someone to do it. It depends upon what he felt, he who threw down the words. There is a great hope in chaos, much less of it in a well-arranged flower-garden. There *has to be* the experiment, it means motion, seed of life and renewal. It *will* be understood by some—and those are the ones to carry innovations over the dark abyss and dead waters and become themselves a seed-bed for that which is called future. Where there is no forward movement, death looms. Therefore people should be grateful that there are those among us who use the costly time of youth to do something completely without rewards, just because they have a song inside. The song can sound bad, but the song purifies itself, as a stream of water cleans itself on the way.[16]

So far Vesaas about the essence of poetry-writing in our time. A reader first confronted with his poetry might feel that Vesaas is more of an experimentalist than he professes to be. Doubtless the element of novelty and immediacy is closely connected with his unorthodox usage of nature imagery. This to a certain degree also makes his poems strangely elusive; students of modern Norwegian literature find them downright difficult, much more so than his novels.

The poetry of the nineteenth and early twentieth century traditionally tells *about* things. The re-creative process required from the reader is relatively easy, since the images behave in a predictable way—what the reader sees before his mental eye is already strongly inherent in the poem, the effect of the poet as a catalyst very much apparent. On the other hand, in most of Vesaas's poems (and in those of many of his contemporaries) things lead a life of their own, the reader confronts them directly rather than the poet's platonic shadow image of them. Once liberated, the concrete image acquires a new function: it is the unpredictable carrier of the author's thoughts and feelings. Thus, in order to create a certain atmosphere the poet has to let the images follow each other in a close succession—concealing himself behind their power of expression. The reader's task is to let the created atmosphere come to life in himself and from there take the step into the abstract world of thoughts. In other words, the reader has to follow a road exactly opposite to that taken by the poet. That this demands much of the reader is obvious. It is also obvious that the result of his endeavors does not necessarily coincide with the author's original feeling. Moreover, it is conceivable that the same object or image might for the poet, depending on mood and situation, be connected with a variety of feelings and thoughts—sometimes even diametrically opposed—which render symbols multivalent, depending on the individual poem. It is probably this trait more than anything else which makes the poems difficult to grasp. Yet, after having read some, one becomes familiar with the poet's techniques.

Not all of Vesaas's poetry is written in this vein. In his first collection, *The Springs,* many poems are rather conventional. Here Vesaas has not yet renounced rhyme and meter. Many poems show an influence from ancient folk ballads, especially in form. And there are many rather romantic idylls of nature and farm life.

A detailed discussion of all six of Vesaas's collections of poetry would lead too far here, keeping in mind also that the last five collections—one of which is *Land of Hidden Fires*—have much in common.[17] *Land of Hidden Fires* was chosen for translation because it seems to reflect best the variety in Vesaas's poetry. Simple poems with a firm rhyme scheme and meter are juxtaposed with poems in truly experimental form, and with poems that are totally philosophical. None of the other collections shows so much change and variety; it is as if in *Land of Hidden Fires* Vesaas created an anthology of those poems he might have felt were most representative of his work.[18]

Land of Hidden Fires—the poems and their translation

Who translates a poet badly
Plays a lackey's role
Grotesquely garbed
In his master's clothes.

GONZÁLES PRADA[19]

The reader must judge how much the translators of the following poems are guilty of this masquerade. In order to give him the opportunity to do so, the corresponding Norwegian text is printed as well. The original text also should be of interest to the reader who does not understand Norwegian. There are many words, especially nouns, in Norwegian that are closely related to their English equivalents: *tre*—tree, *song*—song, *ting*—thing, *hete*—heat, *frost*—frost, *hjarte*—heart, *stjerne*—star are but a few examples.

Moreover, since Norwegian, much like Spanish or German, is a rather phonetic language, even the reader unfamiliar with Norwegian or other Scandinavian languages should be able to respond to the special tone evoked by certain sound-combinations.

All the translations are meant to speak for themselves as poems in their own right. The reader should be aware here that all translations of poems are at the same time interpretations, maybe the closest ones possible since no problem can be evaded or circumnavigated in a translation. For every expression in the original a clear-cut decision has to be made. This is especially difficult in poems where a central set of symbols and imagery oscillates with so many different nuances. Our translations therefore do not necessarily represent grammatically and syntactically correct line-by-line translations of the original; rather, they try to justify the atmosphere and the spirit of the original poem as a whole. We felt free at times to change the outer appearance of a poem, rearrange lines and shorten or lengthen "stanzas." Sometimes the translations suffer from our choice of interpretation, or, at least, they are limited by it. This might be especially true of poems like "Let Dreaming Dogs Lie" and "Heat" (the latter probably being the most problematic poem in the whole collection).

Most of Vesaas's poetic techniques create no problem: it is relatively easy to equate onomatopoeia, alliteration, repetition and an occasional rhyme—all these devices used very often by Vesaas. On the other hand we found we had to modify punctuation, since for American practice most of the poems seemed overpunctuated. There were also problems with words that appear in italics in the original, which are meant to be especially emphatic. Very often these words are pronouns, quite frequently demonstrative. Because the Norwegian demonstrative can have the same form as an article, italics would be justified there, but uncalled for in English. Since in the course of our translation we were forced to shift the emphases slightly, and thus could not hope to duplicate in italics exactly the same words in English as in the original, we decided that it would not damage the English versions too much if we discarded the italics altogether. A third problem has to do with the structure of Norwegian. As in German, an impersonal "it" enjoys extensive usage. The problems of relating impersonal pronouns to the proper noun in the English translation are sometimes almost insurmountable. Yet, once a decision has been made, it necessarily simplifies the poem and often limits ambiguities intended by the poet. Among the more technical difficulties belongs the question of tense. In Norwegian it is acceptable to shift tenses in the same train of thought. In English, a shift of tense may break coherence. A decision often had to be made about what tense to use.

One entire section (section III) of the poems is rhymed. These poems were the most difficult ones to translate. Originally written for a childrens' reader, they are extremely simple, both in composition and style. They have either an uncomplicated form of cross-rhymes or couplets. These seven poems are truly a translator's nightmare. In Norwegian the poems have the classic beauty of a folk ballad or a nursery rhyme in their simplicity. In English there is a danger that any given version may sound trite. It was much worse when we tried to use similar rhyme-schemes that necessarily appeared very contrived. In the end we left out the rhyme, except for an occasional one here and there. For example, many lengthy discussions arose over the poem "First Snow." The poem piles image upon image, expressing the immediacy and the chilling threat of an impending winter, to end laconically with the anticlimactic announcement of winter's arrival: "Then, the winter has come to the North" (literal translation). The last line pulls the rug out from under us. The literal translation of the line, which has a very definite, almost proverbial ring to it in Norwegian, obviously does not do justice to the original. But since the last line seems to have a softening, slightly positive and certainly an ironic tone, we compromised on: "thus winter comes—and goes—up north." We captured the optimistic quality contained in the "going" and the proverbial quality. The ironic element had to be sacrificed, also largely the content of the word "north" which to Scandinavians means their home country.

We also had the problem of rendering Vesaas's nature imagery into English. Norway, with a nature varied and rich in contrasts, has quite a few more words in its language designating natural phenomena than English. Most of these can be expressed quite adequately in English too. Yet some cases are more obstinate: for example, there is simply no word in the English language that has the same scope of meaning as the Norwegian *tele* (basically that layer of earth that remains solidly frozen throughout the winter).

And then there are cultural implications. A word like *boat* means a lot more to a Norwegian than, let's say, to a Midwesterner. The boat is part of his history, his present economy, his transportation, his pleasure. In short, it is a basic concept in his entire culture, charged with traditions and emotions. Similarly, snow-covered mountain tops or even a birch tree are central images. What is a translator to do with this problem? If he wants to be exact, he has to introduce explanatory footnotes—which we feared would detract from the unimpeded enjoyment of each poem.

However, some comments—in lieu of footnotes—may shed light on certain aspects of the poems.

Leafing through the poems and reflecting on the grouping (there are four groups with respectively 16, 9, 7 and 10 poems), somehow *Vigelandsparken* in Oslo comes to mind. It contains a huge collection of sculptures by the Norwegian artist Gustav Vigeland. He was especially interested in the dynamics of the human body. His statues and gigantic arrangements of human bodies bristle with potential energy, usually caught in a posture symbolic of basic human behavior and life. Some of these elements seem inherent also in Vesaas's poems, if we just substitute "soul" for "body." The elemental, stirring forces latent in the human soul are the topical common denominator for many of these poems. And like many of Vigeland's statues, Vesaas's poems too are loosely arranged in four groups reminding one of the "great cycle" of life represented in the four ages of man: childhood, adolescence, maturity, old age, or in the four seasons of the year.

In the first group, poems like "Morning Song under a Tree" or "Still is the Surface" indicate springlike qualities—the morning of the beginning life or the stirring of the hidden forces ready to erupt, but still contained. These two poems are complex both in theme and form. The collection opens with an invitation, a poem that is often used as an opening poem for anthologies of Norwegian poetry. It urges us gently, yet very intensely, to follow. Vesaas literally takes our hand and leads us on. At the same time we are in *medias res,* overwhelmed by nature imagery which, although it decidedly reflects the contrasts typical of Norwegian nature, remains strangely abstract: the *locus* is not really present. This is true of most of Vesaas's poetry. The landscape is Norwegian with its mountains, lakes, coastlines, yet even in the third group of poems which deal more than any others with his native Telemark (place names!) the images are composed of the basic elements in nature (wind, water, earth, sky) and lack the local detail, the local flavor. The poem "Still is the Surface," the key poem of the whole collection, gives the clearest expression of the latent forces (both positive and negative) raging inside us—a theme which provided the name for the entire collection: *Land of Hidden Fires.* The same theme is repeated, now using a different setting, in "Glass under Tension." The shorter poem, "The Living," is technically the best one in the whole collection and it is also most indicative of the basic structural element in Vesaas's poetry: the quick succession of images, not necessarily linked causally, which come to life themselves, creating certain atmospheres and moods. "Perspective," "The Boat on Land," "Footprints," and "Lonely Death" introduce a slightly different aspect of Vesaas's poetry: the problem of human isolation. The most important one of these poems is "The Boat on Land" (his last novel *The Boat in the Evening* is closely related to it). "The Inverted House" takes us one step beyond the problem of mere isolation, it demonstrates the resulting feeling of guilt, of sin against one's neighbor—a matter of perennial concern to Vesaas. "Inscriptions" bears a faint resemblance to the Mosaic tablets of the divine law. The inscriptions here are written in the rich language of nature and bear the age-old message: "Know thyself." "Along the Line" is another poem thematically related to Vesaas's prose, more precisely to his novel *The Signal*. Still another poem, "Clean Dress," in the second group, is related to a novel: *The Bleaching Place*. In form, the first sixteen poems vary from the free verse of "Invitation" to the strong rhyme of "Golden Sand," which also has a consistent rhyme-pattern of couplets. One poem, "Still is the Surface," in its opening resembles the Eddic *fornyrdislag*. Free verse prevails, however, in this group.

After the "spring" poems a smaller group of "summer" poems follows. The seasonal element is indicated in the poem "Summer after Summer," as well as in "June" and in "A Night for Growing." The latter poem is probably the most central one in this group; it deals with the miracle of life itself. *The tree*, Vesaas's most often used symbol of life is found here, as well as the unborn child on whom the whole potential of nature is concentrated. Both "Northgoing" and "Between Breaths" deal with life in a wider sense—in its essence, as a voyage.

The third group contains poems, some of which clearly indicate autumn; for example, in "Mountain Encounter" the herdsmen return from the mountains in fall. "First Snow" is even more obvious. This group of seven poems is separated from the other three by its extreme simplicity of diction. (The poems here were actually written for a childrens' reader.) By their meter and strict rhyme patterns, many of the poems remind us of the traditional folk ballad.

xl

In these poems non-Scandinavians will have to overcome a culture barrier. The imagery used is simple and of a kind which any Norwegian child would be familiar with (the birch tree, the snow, the filly etc.). Most of these poems are permeated with a feeling of security for which children seem to yearn (Gunnar lies in his bed while the birch keeps watch—people are snugly inside while it snows in the mountains). This section, along with some of the poems in section II, is filled with reassuring, consoling moments and hints of answers counter-balancing all the problems expressed in the poems of the first section.

The main issue in the fourth group is death—it is winter, the "days are frosty" and the dog sleeps in front of the fire. The most moving and technically most perfect poem is "Nightwatch," a highly personal poem; Vesaas had the death of his own mother in mind when he wrote it. In other poems the fire which was "under the surface" earlier now breaks forth. In "Burning," it devours and kills, but also purifies and cleans. From here it is apparently a short step for Vesaas to apply this imagery to Christ's passion in the poem "Heat," the longest, most complex and difficult poem of the collection. Any remarks on it here would be confusing rather than enlightening. It will have to be judged on its merits more than the other poems.

It is not surprising that the last poem, "The Bird in the Flame," envisions the Phoenix rising from the ashes. No other logical step could have followed. The collection ends on a positive note, yet with a question:

Do you still cry?
Do you still cry out?

Notes

1. Translations of poems and of prose excerpts in the introduction are mine. The following poems appear with the permission of the author: Tor Jonsson, "Norwegian Love Song"; J. M. Bruheim, "Crossroads," and Tore Ørjasæter, "Night in Oslo." (F. K.)
2. To round out the picture it should be added that there are also parties which support the idea of making one language of the two. Others oppose forcing two languages together artificially.
3. Torbjørn Støverud, *Milestones of Norwegian Literature*, Oslo: Grundt Tanum Forlag, 1967, p. 9.
4. *Tarjei Vesaas, 1897-20. august 1967*, Oslo: Gyldendal Norsk Forlag, 1967.
5. Ibid., p. 1.
6. Ibid., p. 27.
7. Ibid., p. 72.
8. One should not, however, overlook the autobiographical aspects of his works, especially his novel *The Great Cycle* (1934).
9. Tarjei Vesaas, "Om skrivaren," in *Ei bok om Tarjei Vesaas* av Ti Nordiske Studentar, ed. Leif Mæhle, Oslo: Det Norske Samlaget, 1964. This essay is the basis of the following biographical sketch.
10. Ragnvald Skrede, *Tarjei Vesaas*, Oslo: Gyldendal Norsk Forlag, 1947.
11. Kenneth G. Chapman, *Tarjei Vesaas*, New York: Twayne Publishers, 1970. Biographical data for Vesaas's later years are drawn from this source.
12. Vesaas, "Om skrivaren," p. 26.
13. Ibid., p. 26.
14. Ibid., p. 28. See also Harald S. Næss's critical estimate in his introduction to *The Great Cycle*, trans. Elizabeth Rokkan, Madison: University of Wisconsin Press, 1962.
15. Kresten Nordentoft, "The Themes," in *Ei bok om Vesaas*, p. 66. For a brief summation of Vesaas's accomplishment as a novelist, see Philip Houm, *Norges Litteratur fra 1914 til 1920 årene*, Oslo: Aschehoug & Co., 1955, 6:246.
16. Vesaas, "Om skrivaren," pp. 27-28.
17. See Yngvil Molaug Stang's essay on Vesaas's lyric poetry, "Lyrikken," in *Ei bok om Tarjei Vesaas*, esp. p. 271; and Harald Beyer, *Norsk Litteratur Historie*, Oslo: H. Aschehoug & Co., 1963, p. 439.
18. In the meantime a short anthology of Vesaas's poems has appeared with introduction: Kenneth G. Chapman, *Tarjei Vesaas, 30 Poems*, Oslo: Universitetsforlaget, 1971.
19. Translated by William M. Davis in *An Anthology of Spanish Poetry from Garcilaso to García Lorca*, ed. Angel Flores, Garden City, N.Y.: Doubleday, 1961.

Land of Hidden Fires I

Innbying

Vil du gje meg handa ved månens skin,
lauv du er—
Under open himmel. Over open avgrunn.

Som lauv
er du og eg.
Fort skjelvande,
og fort borte.
Kom—

Invitation

Will you give me your hand in the moonlight,
you are leaves . . .
Under open sky. Over the yawning precipice.

Like leaves,
you and I.
Trembling in the wind
and quickly gone.
Come . . .

Morgonsong ved treet

Frå dei yttarste kvistene
strøymer angane,
strøymer sorglaust ut i vinden
som frå vakre hender.
Fargeflekker lagar seg
på alle tre
i heite ynske,
så fuglane i lufthavet svingar av,
så dei ikkje kjem lenger
for sin eigen frambrytande song.

Kvinneleg frå øvst til nedst.
Treet står nakent under borken
og let sevjene sile.
Frå marka går beiske kraftstrenger
opp i den innarste søten.
I mørke jordlag
opnast nye brunnar utan stans
for fjerne himmelkroner.

Fløyd alle kjelder, fløyd.
Drikk drikk, alt liv.

Morning Song under a Tree

From the outstretched branches
fragrance flows,
floats playfully away on the wind,
as tossed from slender hands.
Waves of color drift luringly
over the reaching limbs,
enticing the birds in oceans of air,
to sink to the branches
and sing.

Feminine from top to toe.
She stands nude beneath her bark
and lets her naked juices flow.
From below, bitter roots
probe her inner sweetness.
In dark layers of soil
deeper wells open
to nourish still taller trees
that crown the horizon.

Flow, springs, flow. Drink,
drink, all that lives.

Still er yta

Still er yta
i eldars land,
ingen ting viser,
det er jamvekt alt.

Men ting i gang
i denne stund
som heite ras
i indre fjell.
Dei veit det, dei få
som har sett gjennom revnene
og kjent heten slå.

Menneske dregst til menneske
i eldhunger over tusen mil
—og er straks ikkje uvisse lenger,
auga til auga
og for einannen, om sanninga om
eldens djup og eldars ville møte.

Still is the Surface

Still is the surface
in the land of fire,
nothing shows: everywhere
balance.

But underneath:
sudden stirring,
molten avalanches
rumbling in the mountain's heart.
They knew the few
who peered between the cracks
and felt the throbbing heat.

Man drawn to man
across a thousand miles
as if thirsting for a single flame—
as soon no longer doubts
—when face to face
and for the other, the truth
of the fire's vast depth
and the fierceness of its burning.

Gullsand

Straumen stri gjennom lendet går,
djup og u-skir frå år til år.

Lendet er hjartet med søkk og sving.
Straumen er kostbare livsens ting.

Straumen slår støkt imot trollvegg glatt.
Straumen renn sælt kvar fredens natt.

Straumen hindrast av urett gram.
I kjærleiks dal flyt han mektig fram.

Straumen skyler blant grums og stein.
Botnens gullsand blir vaska rein.

Grann etter grann gjer forma full.
Slik blir det til, det hjartegull.

Golden Sand

A stream courses through the heart of the land
And through the land of the heart over stone and sand

With twists and turns through the land and the heart
The current plays a vital part

The currents pound on the wall of the troll
Yet on peaceful evenings both placidly flow

Though the currents are hindered by adversity
In the valley of love they run rapidly

And from the rocks they spill between
They wash the golden grains of the bottom clean

And thus is formed from the very start:
The heart of gold, and the gold of the heart.

Auga i natta

Står du enno som ein blind
under stjerner?
Men den søkande er etter deg.

Stjernene vandrar i sikre baner,
som dei styrde Heimen,
uendeleg langt over all søking
over all lengt
og over all ve.
Men den søkande søker for det,
kvar kjøleg stjernekveld.

Evig går han ut av huset sitt og spør
om meininga med gråten, med krigen,
med synd mot nesten, med all eiga fornedring
som ikkje er å stå imot.

Kvar kjøleg stjernekveld.
Han søker,
og før eller seinare slår han ned på deg
med sin brann
og får deg tend.
Slitande sug skal bli kveikt i deg ved møtet.
Din gode fred på putene vil kverve.
Heitare og heitare vil auga ditt vake i mørkret.

Eyes in the Night

Do you still blindly stand
beneath the stars—
when the Searcher pursues you?

Stars follow certain paths,
as if they ruled the World,
above all searching
above all longing
above all pain.
But the Searcher searches
each cool and starry night.

He forever leaves his house and humbly asks
the why of tears, of war,
of sins against one's neighbor.

Every cool and starry night
He searches, and soon or late
descends on you with his fire
and sets you aflame.
This fire will kindle a fearful blaze,
destroying your peace on the pillows,
and your burning eyes
will stay awake in the dark.

Spent glas

Det glimtar i halvmørkret
frå ei sliping i pokalen.
Der brytinga i glaset
lagar lyn.

Han står der i fest-tummel.
Ingen rører han,
spend og farleg, av glas.
Ingen vågar lyfte han
om dei aldri så gjerne ville.
I denne tummel av
natt og fest,
der tungt blod er i sig.

For i denne stunda
ville eit grep
kring glaset gleppe,
dei fest-sveitte fingrane glide,
den isande pokalen brake i golvet
—og spenninga i han lage han
til glitrande dust.

Romsamt blir det av den grunn
der han no står oppstilt
og dyl si dødsens spenning.
Den kjølege yta skaper tomrom
som for lurande fare.

Glass under Tension

The goblet's polished crystal
sparkles in the twilight,
where refractions in the glass
sprinkle, splinters of light.

Amidst the festive bustle
it stands
poised.
No one touches it.
Brittle and fragile glass.
No one dares lift it,
though many are tempted.
In the bustle
of night and joy
where thick blood is seeping.

For in this instant
the grip on glass
would be lost,
the fingers—damp with revelry—slip,
the icy goblet shatter to the floor—
its tension turning
to glittering dust.

The goblet stands
in empty space
and hides its deadly tension.

Fare er det ikkje,
men det klare og useielege
ein berre veit om og ville ha.

Tungt blod i sig–
på morgonkanten.
Og andlet vil ikkje møtast med andlet
på morgonkanten,
men hender skjelv og leitar
og hender finn fram over alt,
ublygt og tyrst.
Klamme og heite veit alle hender samstundes
at det var ikkje *dette*, men det andre,
det andre og atter det andre,
som dei ville halde og ha som sitt
—men braket over alle brak
ringer varslande i tomromet
på førehand.

Its chilly surface creates a vacuum
as if luring to danger.
But there is no danger.
Only the crystal-clear and the inexpressible;
only knowledge and desire.

Thick blood seeps—
at the break of day.
And face will not meet face—
at the break of day.
But hands will tremble and grope
and hungry hands find everything
that hands can hold.
Moist and warm, the hands know:
It wasn't this, but that,
that, which they longed to hold
and keep—
but the echo of other shatterings
sounds a forewarning
in the empty space.

Dei levande

Kvelden er ein haustkveld og kvesser sine knivar.
Stjernene blir høge og husa våre varme.
Nakne er vi skapte og natta er vår eiga.

Frosten bur i natta og telen bur i jorda.
Elden bur i menneske og skifter ikkje bustad.
Hjarte bur i natta mellom roser.

The Living

The evening, the fall evening whets its knives.
The stars gain height and our houses warmth.
Naked are we created and the night is ours.

The chill lives in the night and the frost lives in the
       earth.
The fire lives in man and seeks no other house.
The heart lives in the night between roses.

Spennvidder

Dei store tårnklokkene,
dei store stormane,
dei store roparane,
har lita spennvidd.
Spennvidd har *du*
i dine løyndrom.

Dei framande bårene der
har for lenge sidan gjort deg
lykkeleg og redd.
Dei framande bårene der
skyler til nakne grunnen,
reinskar for slam,
dynger grus over att,
og når lenger enn din fugl kan fly.

Om du skjøna alt du er med på
som ein del av båreslaget—
Du kjenner berre torsten og slitinga
og kvila og angesten og lykka,
etter som du svingar.

Perspective

The screaming bells
The screaming seas
The screaming voices
have little reach. But
You have reach—
within.

The strange waves there
wash wordlessly over earth,
rinse from it the mud,
re-cover it with sand—
reaching further than the reach of thought.
The strange waves there
have long since left you
happy—and afraid?
Reaching further than the reach of thought.

If you only understood that all your thoughts
are moved by the waves' roll . . .
But you only see the peace, the pain,
the fear, the joy,
depending on what catches the eye.

Båten ved land

Din stille båt
har ikkje namn.
Din stille båt
har ikkje hamn.
Din gøymde båt ved land.

For dette er då ikkje hamnen—
Lauvet blikar i vårnettene
oppover den ventande ferdige båten,
og drys gult og vått
nedover toftene i oktober,
og ingen har vori her.

Men her finst sog ifrå endelause
sletter av sjø,
der soler går opp av djupet
og vinden går mot hamnen bakom.

Men det er heller ikkje hamnen,
anna ein stad med sog og kalling
frå endå større sletter,
større storm i strendene,
og ein større båt om kvelden.

Din stille båt
gror langsamt ned.
Din gøymde båt ved land.

The Boat on Land

You, resting boat,
have no name.
You, harborless boat,
are hidden on land.

For this is no haven—
above the waiting ready boat
the leaves shimmer in the spring night
and fall in October golden and wet
on the hull—
no one has been there.

But here is the gulping sound of an endless sea
suns rising from the depths
and wind blowing toward the harbor.

But neither is this the true harbor;
only another dawning world
with a still bigger sea,
with a still bigger storm blowing on the beaches—
a still bigger boat in the evening.

Your resting boat,
overgrowing slowly
is hidden on the land.

Sporet

På den bortløynde sandstranda er
der ingen lenger.
Over står berga forbrende.

Ein sandboge, bittert forleten,
full av eit einaste spor! forleten,
fråflydd etter bresteferdig venting.

Over står berga forbrende.
Noken har vori her
og gått og gått
—men over *dette* vatnet kom det ingen.

Sanden var berre innramma av underlege berg.
Den gule sanden
med sine siste einsame spor.

Hastig samanrasa spor.
Tallause søkk i sanden berre.
Vandringa av din unge fot i vilske,
dine mjuke steg, i torste, før du flydde.
Din beste draum for ingen.
Din gylne skapnad bortspilt.

Footprints

No one comes anymore
to the forgotten beach—
Above stand the sunburnt rocks.

Left behind—
a stretch of beach,
with a single footprint—
left after anxious waiting.

Above stand the sunburnt rocks
Where someone has been
and walked
and walked . . .
but no one came over this water.

The beach framed in ghostly rocks.
Last lonely prints
in the yellow sand.

Countless footprints faintly made.
Depressions in the sand.
Aimless wandering of soft wishful steps
before you fled. Your fondest dream
—for nothing.
Your sunripe form—wasted.

Herlege evner for ingen ingen
—medan dei svarte bergsidene stod over
med grimer i draga
frå tidlegare liv.

Precious gifts for nothing, no one . . .
While the dark rocks stand above
with wrinkled faces
from earlier lives.

Død einsam

Enno enno
har ingen komi—

Glaset er oppe.
Svarte fluger surrar ut og inn.
Det sit ei fluge urørleg på eit kinn.

Dørene oppe mot vindane,
så vindar kan gå som dei vil.
Men her
er ikkje vindane til.

Fåfengt—
men alt her er opna mot det brusande!
Det var den siste underlege gjerning,
den siste klare viljen som blinka i romet
før skodda la seg ned
fylt av mørke songrøyster,

men som ikkje var songrøyster
anna flugene flugene—

Lonely Death

Still . . . still
no one comes—

The window is open.
Black flies buzz in and out.
One sits motionless on a cheek.

The doors are open to the winds
that they may come and go.
But here none blow.

But all here was open to the raging storm.
In vain—
It was the last grand act,
the last clear thought
which flashed and flickered in the room
before dusk fell
filled with singing, dark voices.

But which were not voices singing
only flies, flies . . .

Huset på tvers

Punktet i natta
er eit stort hus
fullt av slæpande,
basta og bundi
til si tunge svill
—mykje skulle vi gje
for at ikkje det var til.

Alltid det huset på tvers.
Med tunge saker tenkt inn der.
Alt som i grunnen er *vårt*.
For det er vi som skulle vori der,
synest vi stadig.
Vi skulle teki børene
og sveitten.

Som skuldmenn går vi framom
fordi vårt liv vart lettare.
Det svarte punktet ligg der og blir mørkare.
Huset der dei slit med
det vi skulle sliti.
Der *vi* har det opnande ordet.
Men ordet har vi kasta i ein brunn.

Framom så hastig.
Vi veit det så tydeleg
alt som går for seg

The Inverted House

A speck in the night—
A big house
packed with toiling workers,
tied and tethered
to their heavy yoke.
Much would we give
if it were not so.

Always this inverted house.
The heavy thoughts within.
All of which belongs to us, as well.
Always thinking,
we ought to be there, too.
We should have taken on the load
and the sweat.

Like debtors, we go on
as life becomes easier
and the black speck grows darker.
Where they do the work
that should have been ours.
There we have the opening word.
But we have thrown the word into a well.

We rush on.
We know too well
all that goes on

og auga slår vi ned:
Kjøvande luft der. Strimer i andletet.
Dødtrøytt svevn der
med sin gløymsel.

Framom der endå ein gong.
Skjert anar vi vår vanmakt.
Mykje skulle vi bytte av tida vår
imot kraft og kjærleik.
Mykje skulle vi gje av tid
for å orke seia ordet.
Men ordet ligg på botnen av ein brunn.

and drop our eyes:
the choking air. The faces
the dead-tired sleep
that rinses memory.

We rush on
and cannot cope.
We should barter years
for strength and love.
We should gladly give those years
if only we could say the word
But the word lies at the bottom of a well.

Innskriftene

Klårast lyser innskrifter
som det er eld i:
Sanninga om brorskap på jorda
står og lyser—
Lygna kring krigen blir skjerande avdekt.
Teiknet på alles ansvar
står og i glod.

Klårast lyser innskriftene
i atom-tider
—som er frukt av neveslag gjennom tusen år.
Våre tusen uvennlege små gjerningar.
Alle har vi dyrka ei lita dødsens kjerne.

Klårast lyser innskriftene
som vi blundar for.
Dei les vi i mørkret
når vi skulle sova.

Inscriptions

Brightest shine the inscriptions
written in fire: the truth
of brotherhood glows white-hot; the lie
of war is forced into light.
Man's debt, branded,
flames higher.

Brightest shine the inscriptions
in atomic ages—the climax
of fainter blows struck through thousands of years.
Our thousand bitter, petty deeds—
We have all sown death with tiny seeds.

Brightest shine the inscriptions
to which we close our eyes.
These we read in the dark
when we should sleep.

Høgstdag

I høgstdagen får du ikkje låne skugge
om himmelens sol har spjut.
Og duren under jorda
er for deg å stanse!
blir det ropt seint og tidleg.

Du med ungdoms bitre søte ring
i minnet
—då ein kyss var eit under
og ei hand ein draum—
kvar er du no?
Det ropar på deg og
din manndom.
Det ropar,
og din harde kjake knytest.

Du i din høgstdag,
du som skal og skal og skal.
Som skal møte duren under jorda,
binde stutar som har sliti seg,
finne svalande kjelder,
skaffe barn ting å tru på
—og som skal kunne le
når alt samen synest rådlaust.

Noon

At noon you find no refuge in the shade
when the sun hurls spears.
And you are endlessly commanded:
Still the rumbling in the earth.

You with the bitter-sweet youth
ringing in your memory
—when kisses were miracles still
and a hand, a dream—
where are you now?
You and your manhood
are commanded—
a call—and
your knuckles turn white.

you in your noon time
you shall you shall you shall.
You shall overcome the rumbling in the earth,
pen the straying bull,
find soothing springs,
create things a child can believe
—but you will be able to laugh
when all else seems futile.

Langs linja

Her ligg han,
han som ville lokomotiv.
Som ville jarnsider,
og ras mot eit einaste målpunkt.
Her var det altsamen for hans draum.

Alt ein vil kan ein få
når ein ikkje vil meir enn lokomotiv.
Hendene kviler heite av lyst
på blankt stål i finslipt form,
og skjønar ikkje kva hender er til.

Lokomotivet skyt eld framfor seg
så snart det er mørkt.
Lokomotivet køyrer i natta med eitt auga,
som i gudars visdom.
Her ligg han for tidleg kald, han som tilbad det.

Kva er skjedd?
Kva veit vi om kva han fekk visst
av visdomen
innan det var slutt?
Vi er folk langs linja, berre,
og lokomotivet dyn kvar tid
framom våre kjære.

Along the Line

Here lies one
who wanted a locomotive,
wished for sides of steel,
and an open throttle
toward some single aim.
Here was everything
needed for his dream.

And everything one desires, one can have (if
one wants no more than a locomotive)
for hands lie hot with longing
on smooth and shining steel—
and soon forget what hands are for.

And the engine spouts its fire in the night
slicing the darkness with a single eye—
like the wisdom of gods.
Here he lies
too soon cold.
He who longed for a locomotive.

What happened?
What do we know, how can we surmise
of what he came to know or realize
before it was too late?
We can only stand along the line,
the engine roaring, always,
past the ones we love.

Vi fyller dei vidaste nettene

Glatt er glasberget:
eit sjølvlysande berg om kvelden,
eit glinsande berg av heilskap,
i dei underlege nettene
nede ved foten av det,
der *vi* er.

Her alt er alt, kan du
ikkje vera lenge,
du som er samansett av halvt og ulikt,
og menneske av kjøt og veikskap
—her er det inga forståing.
Men det seier i deg: eg vil.
Det seier oppatt og utruleg at eg vil.

Tallause er vi
alle som vil vera her.
Alle som vil
trass alt vi gjer.
Vi fyller dei vidaste nettene.
Og vårt ørvesle sjølvlysande grann
blir samanlagt som ei ljosskodd
lågt nede ved marka
—ved det store berget
der inga forståing finst.

We Fill the Deepest Nights

The glass mountain is smooth:
luminous in the evening,
a shining peak of perfection
in the wonderous night:
down, at its foot—
we stand.

We cannot stand here
where all is all,
we who are joined
in unequal halves
and man of flesh and failing
—here is no understanding.
But a voice within is saying: I want;
keeps saying: "I want."

Legion are we,
who want to be
here, who want
in spite of all our deeds.
Filling the deepest nights.
And our tiny, shining being
defuses in a dome of light
close to the earth—
close to the mountain
where there is no understanding.

II

I Midtbøs bakkar

Har alle varme regnskur gjort deg ør?
Det har dei ved stilla innimellom,
med brå-sol, toreluft, og gutar
som *dine* blomar lokkar fram.
For det blømer i Midtbøs bakkar så vi er ville.
Her rykker i rota og vil danse.
Her er tusen fleir enn vi tenkte.
Kvar levedag er det
annleis enn det var før.

Ikkje noko namn for det som går
forma som gjente i ei eng,
hitover hitover, ør av veret,
aldri pusta på av menner,
blindt komande i si bløming.
Dette er dagen for bløming, gjente,
med heit sol på våte lemer
og med dunkande vandring
mot det du ikkje får.

Svalt laver du av dogg.
Enga rekk oppetter deg
og vaskar deg med kaldare
som gjer deg fast.
Glitrande av væte kjem du fram att or graset
frå topp til tå
—og der i solbeltet, i bråvarmen,

On Midtbø's Hills

Have all the warm showers made you giddy?
Sometimes—in the stillness,
the surprise of sudden sun,
the pause of thunder—hanging
in the air,
and the flocking of young men
summoned by your flowers.
Their blooming leaves us breathless,
as they quiver to the core
and long to dance.
More than we thought, so many more
and different, somehow different,
than before.

Nameless is that which strides, girl-like,
in a meadow, closer,
nearer,
made giddy by the air too rarefied
for men—
blindly growing, blindly blooming.
This is the day for blooming, girl—
burning sun on moist limbs
and a fevered wandering
toward something you can never find,
or finding, keep.

You shine with cool dew
and the meadow reaches up

mellom skurene og toreslaga,
ligg ormen og øver seg i hogg.

Mange øver seg i mangt.
I skur-regn og tore og dampande gras
vil du møte det og bli trolla av det,
om det så er ein svart blom.
Du vil aldri sleppe usåra frå Midtbøs bakkar
og di blømings tid.
Som du sjølv vil bli eit spel for noken,
vil din draum og bli eit spel for noken,
når det dimmest over enga og lid langt.

and splashes you with colder dew
that braces you.
Glittering with wetness
you emerge from the grass
—and there is a flash of sun,
between the thunderclaps,
in the sudden heat—
The snake suns himself and lies in wait
and practices his striking.

In showers and storms and steaming grass
you will stumble upon it—spellbound—
as by a black flower.
You will never come untouched, unharmed
from Midtbø's hills
and your time of blooming.
As you will, for some
become a prey
your dream, as well, for some
becomes mere play
when it grows dark over the meadow
and the day grows late.

Stilna brud

Angen frå alle mine somrar
er i kransen kring mitt hår,
er dette alt?

Så få og forte!
så useielege var mine stutte somrar,
med bortgøymd sevje
og med trå.

I kveld dirrar lampene i dansen.
Min kveld som brud—
Sjå salens auge søker,
kvar eg står,
og salens auge syg.
Min dirr er duld.
Min fot har hastig stilna.
Min krans—
min krans er tung.

The Quiet Bride

The scent of all my summers
hangs wreathed about my hair
is this all?

How few, how fast—
beyond all words were my summers
with hidden desires
and longing.

Tonight, my night,
lamps tremble in the dance—
Here I stand where every eye
takes me in a glance—everything,
except my trembling dread.
My steps have slowed quickly.
My wreath—my wreath
hangs heavy upon my head.

Sommar etter sommar

Atter attende—
sommar etter sommar.
Kva jagast her?

Kva jagast her?
Linnea i granskogen?
Minnet om svirpen av ein kjole?
Badet i bekken som såg din ungdom?

Men framande er no i graset.
Stråa nikkar sakte.
Gå stilt forbi.
Gå bort.

Ja stråa nikkar sakte,
sommar etter sommar,
og sprukken jord gaper
—for her var du gut og
brann opp,
og dei mjuke svalande leppene
kom aldri hit.

Summer after Summer

Again and again
summer after summer,
pursuing what?

Pursuing what?
The twin flower deep in the pine forest?
The memory of a dress's rustle?
Bathing in the brook
which saw your youth?

But strangers are now in the grass.
The blades nod slowly.
Pass by quietly. Pass
on.

Yes the blades nod slowly,
summer after summer,
and the parched earth yawns
—because here
you were boy
and burning fire
but the soft, cooling lips
came never here.

Rein kjole

Sommarkjolen fyllest av rund kveldvind
og daskar på snora.
Graset nedunder er grønt og stilt,
for vinden er ikkje der.
Ingen ting er dette: raude prikkar
og ein rund vind.
Kjenn angen:
Bortvaska alt det sulk,
att er lin.

Clean Dress

The summer dress is filled with evening breeze
and sways on the line.
The grass beneath is green and still,
no wind is there.
Nothing to speak of: red dots
and a round breeze.
Smell the scent . . .
washed away is all the dirt,
left is linen.

Nordover—

Ingen veit det enno
at det har endra seg.
Ingen veit det enno
at alt er nytt,
at ringen min no går vidare
og kjennest veldig stor,
eller at kroppen min kviskrar sjå på meg,
sjå på meg
no spelar eg for fullt.

Mellom frukt og vin og gyllen kveiteåker
var det at eg vakna såleis.
I eit framandt sudland kviskra min nye kropp,
slo nye tankar ned,
og eg lo, for om eit framandt rike
så var det som sider av meg no.

Ein del av meg er ho heretter,
den jord der dette skjedde.
Di eiga vaksne dotter vil eg kalla meg,
du nye mor, du bjarte sudland, som såleis førebur
i visdom
dei komande hendingar i nord.

For denne di vaksne dotter er på ferd.
Og ingen veit enno kva det kviskra i meg.
Og ingen veit enno kva eg såg,

Northgoing

No one knows yet
that things have changed.
No one knows yet
that everything is new,
that my circle widens
and overwhelms
or that my body whispers: look at me
look at me
now I live with all that's in me.

I woke up thus
among fruit and wine
and golden wheatfields
in a foreign southern land,
my body whispered.
Struck with new flashes
and I laughed, because even though
a foreign land
it was part of me now, the ground
on which I stand.

Your ready daughter,
I will call myself, new mother,
bright, southern country,
you foretell what is to come
up north.

og ingen veit enno kva eg skjønar.
Men eg er på ferd nordover—
Nordover nordover, i stille jubel
over det som noken ukjend skal få visst:
min sæle vokster.
Nordover nordover
—noken enno ukjend
ventar på meg, i si undring,
i mitt gamle land.

Because this one, your
daughter,
is on her way.
And no one knows yet
what was whispered within me.
And no one knows yet what I saw
and what I understand.
But I'm on my way up north—northward
humbly proud of that
which someone yet unknown
will come to know:
my happy growing
—northward, northward—
Someone yet unknown
waits for me,
to be surprised
in my old country.

Juni

Fine legger vætest
i nattgras.
Lutande langstrå vaknar uventa,
stryk av seg dogga
mot forbifarande kne.
Ein søt løyndom.

Tre lette slag på dørkarmen,
i sakte hast,
i trolldoms natt.
Ein leande munn:
er eg sein?

Vått av dogg er mitt hold,
og angar,
og kroppen min ein blome
innfor deg.

June

Slender legs become wet
in the night grass.
Long, leaning blades wake unexpectedly,
brushing their dew
against passing knees.
A sweet secret.

Three light taps on the door
in tender haste,
in the magic of the night.
Smiling lips:
am I late?

Wet with dew are my limbs
and fragrant—
and my flesh a flower
within you.

Det var vi

Det var vi som ropte på sommaren
—og sommarens prestekragar
nikka straks på bakken.
Og det var vi som ropte, framleis,
mot noko vi ikkje visste,
men i torste og lengsel,
og der vi sprang som lange barn
stod enno spor i graset
for så nyleg kjendest *det.*

Og no—
allting så forvirrande,
så brå utruleg, og så kasta omeinannen:
I ein kvit hegg sat far min no
som ung gut, oppkliven, og drøymde om gjenter
—eg vart klumsa og lykkeleg over
korleis han såg ut!
Og samstundes, inne blant prestekragane,
sat eg, og la ei redd og sæl hand
på det varme kneet ditt.
Ei mindre og mindre redd hand.

Du sa ikkje eit ord om alt du skjøna og såg
ifrå di kvinneside
ved at tida ikkje fanst
og ved at botnen æste.
Du svara meg berre utydeleg om handa:
ho lyt få—

It Was We

It was we who summoned summer
and the daisies nodded on the ground.
And it was we who in our longing
summoned something nameless,
something faceless, something strange,
and where we ran as lanky children
there still are tracks in the grass—
where we passed.

And now
everything is blurred . . .
my father, young, sleepless, dreaming
of girls—in a white blooming tree—
and me—delighted yet disturbed
to see the way he looked.
And then, again among the daisies,
I sat, and laid a timid, eager hand
upon your knee—
a less and less timid hand.

And you said nothing,
could say nothing of what you felt:
that for you time had
stopped
and that your depths were stirred.
All you answered, in a touch, was
We.
Then waves, once smooth, grew rough

Slakke bylgjer vart krappare.
Men her gjekk verre rykk enn som så,
enn det vi
ved vårt kunne kalle til live.

Djupare skjelvingar var komme i gang,
kom utanfrå og gjekk inn i oss
og tok oss bort.
Det store ord om alltid fornying,
det store ord om forgreining til det minste,
det store ord om samanhengen,
trass einsemd og atter einsemd,
fekk munn og kunne tala sjølv og voks til storm
—så munnen din vart stum som min,
og våre eigne bårer andres.

and worse tremors shook us
than we could stir.

Wider tides were born,
washed over us,
sweeping us aside.
And despite loneliness,
our loneliness.
The word,
—universal
—eternal
found a mouth,
and was able to speak,
and grew to a storm—
your mouth, like mine,
grew dumb
and our waves, too, became
a tide for others.

Voksternatt

Det er voksternatt og ingen talar.
Du du! kunne det bli sagt,
men det seiest ikkje det eingong
når alt hjå ein kjenner og veit.

Ute er berga oppvermde og metta
av ein kvorven dag,
står bakom og pustar varmen ut att,
som vokstervarme til djupgrønt land,
så den ljodlause voksteren kan halde ved.

Det som skal vekse, veks:
Graset. Trea. Barnet ingen ser.
Dei mørke fjellsidene breier ut med klokskap
i natta
varmen dei har lånt seg
—du du låner av ingen,
legge handa på deg i mørkret
er ikkje berre som å legge henne på
glattslipte solvermde strandsteins-kuv,
det er å legge henne undrande
på liv og mjukleik.

A Night for Growing

It is a night for growing
—not for words.
You . . . you . . . could be said, instead
we say nothing.
—We feel
and know, within.

Outside the mountains, warmed
and mellowed by the dying day,
breathe out the warmth again-
for deep-green growth,
so the silent growing
can go on.

That which shall grow, grows:
The grass. The trees.
The unborn child.
The wise mountains
return the warmth
they've only borrowed.
—You borrow from no one.
To lay a hand on you in the night,
unlike touching sun-baked rocks,
is to feel the warmth
of life.

Mellom andedraga

Innsjøen andar i natt
og lyfter litt på sine strandmål.
Engskodd fortel at enga andar samstundes,
på sin måte,
og søtar anden sin med kløver.
Og gjentene i lia
pustar stutt som mellom sprang, og gror, og søtar
anden sin med seg sjølv.
—Må *ditt* overskot ande og dine kjelder springe,
blant denne livsens lykke,
og bera deg som ei våg gjennom tronge sund,
og vera fullt med, både der åsane over
er mørke og botnane umælte,
og der grunnen lyser opp til fararen
med gul sand og laugeplass,
og der dei vakre holmane er tusen,
så ein liten sjø går sælt vill imellom dei.
Må alt du har
vera med og kjenne,
før det er for seint:
Det syg frå osen,
straumen ligg i vatnet
som bylgjande hår.

Between Breaths

The lake exhales tonight,
raising a little its waterline.
The haze on the meadow tells
that the meadow is breathing, too,
sweetening its breath with clover.
And the girls on the hillsides
pant in short breaths—growing
and sweetening their breath with themselves.
—May your spirit flourish
and your sources flow
in joyful celebration
and carry you like a wave through this narrow sound
to the very marrow, to the heart of things,
while the dark hills are still far-off
and the bottoms of seas are yet unmentioned
—and there
where the bottom is clear to the traveler
and shimmers with yellow sand and shoals,
where the tiny, jewel-like islands
number thousands, this little lake is almost lost
among them—
May all you are be in this,
feel, while still there's time:
the swelling flow, the current
lying in the water like waving hair,
and washing out to sea.

III

Natta, Gunnar og bjørka

Månen skin blankt bak veggen.
Bjørka lyser i leggen.

Bjørka står einsleg ute.
Sløkt er i Gunnars rute.

Bjørka vader i enga.
Barn Gunnar søv godt i senga.

Ingen kan Gunnar taka,
bjørka vil stå og vaka.

The Night, Gunnar and the Birch Tree

The moon shines brightly outside the walls.
The birch tree has white legs.

The birch stands in the dark.
Gunnar's window is dark.

The birch goes wading in the meadow.
Little Gunnar sleeps tight in his bed.

No one can come and harm you.
The birch stands watch over you.

Ketil

Det er ein stad ved vegen
der ein torstedrikk får.
Det er hos gamle Ketil
med det snøkvite hår.

Du støkk vel over torsten
på den villande veg.
Då møter gamle Ketil
med stolprande steg.

Old Ketil

There is a place on the dusty road, where
one can quench a burning thirst—

Old Ketil's place.
He, with snow-white hair.

Parched by your thirst
each step of the way—

Then you meet old Ketil.
He, with his tottering step.

Møtet på fjellet

Rart var det første blad
einsame fjellmenn fekk sjå
då dei kom ned frå svad.

Månadslang stiring i stein
og så utan varsel: eitt kjærteikn
forma som blad på grein.

Kvar ein hadde stygt i sitt blod.
Kvar ein hadde rov i sin hug.
Gripne, ved bladet dei stod.

Mountain Encounter

Disturbing was the first leaf
solitary herdsmen came upon
as they came down barren slopes.

Month-long staring at stones
and then
a touch—
a leaf trembling on a twig.

Each had taint in his blood
each had malice in mind
and still they stood,
shaken by a leaf.

Første snø

Lufta står stiv og still.
Høgt sigler hauken av jakt.
Vinters dag stundar til.

Roleg kvart hus blir eit feste:
vender sin mur imot frost.
Vilt byrjar snøskya breste.

Snart går det første spor
over vårt kvitna tun.
Så er her vinter i Nord.

First Snow

The air stands stiff and still,
high sails the hawk,
hunting—
a winter day begins.

Silently each house becomes a fortress,
turns its walls against the chill—
savagely the snowclouds lash out.

Soon the first prints
lead over the white yard.
Thus winter comes—
and goes—
up north.

På Haukeli alle inne

Snøen snøen snøen
skimrar i nattmørkt skar.
Hjelper i blinde siste vandrar
så han kan sjå sitt far.

Elden elden elden!
brår fram i venleg gavl.
Gangen og lengslene endar ljuvleg
bortanfor gjennomstridd skavl.

Stega stega stega
står i den djupe snø
einslege att inni Dyreskar
der ingen sitt liv skal blø.

Everyone Indoors on Haukeli Mountain

The snow, the snow
shines in the pitch-dark pass.
Unwittingly helps the last wanderer
to see his path.

The light, the light
shines invitingly around the eaves.
The wandering and longing ends
after the struggle through the endless snow.

The steps, the steps
imprinted in the drifting snow
are lonely back in the mountain pass
where no one shall suffer death.

I istida

Fonna ligg over laugevatnet,
over kvart sommarens spor.
Tokke og Bora frå kvite vidder
renn isgrøne ned mot sin fjord.

Men ungdom og ungdoms draumar
blømer på ville vis:
Lagar sin eigen heite sommar
midt i den kvilande is,

har seg eit hemmeleg vassdrag,
oppdelt i ugreitt nett,
set i gang strie varme elvar
ingen har høyrt eller sett.

In the Ice Age

The snowdrift lies on frozen waters
where we swam last summer;
Tokke and Bora from white plateaus
run ice-green down to their fjord.

But youth and the dreams of youth
still thrive,
making their own live thaw
in the ice-grip.

In secret springs below,
they branch out in silent flows,
rushing in warm rivers
no one has seen
or heard.

Stutt er folars flygelov

Klink klink, hestesko.
Klink i stein på furemo.

Stamp stamp, hestefot.
Bakken ber deg tungt imot.

Flyg flyg, folehov!
Stutt er folars flygelov.

The Filly's Time for Flying

Klunk, klunk, horseshoe.
Klunks on rock in a forest of pine.

Stamp, stamp, horsefoot;
The ground is hard to cover,
rises heavily up against you.

Fly, fly, filly's hoof.
Brief is the filly's time for flying.

IV

Garnsund

Ein seinkveld sig garnet i sundet.
Spent over sundet
i småregn og skuming,
gøymt nedi botnen
så ingen ting viser.
Båten kjem stille og mannen er tagal,
og mannen i båten gjer stum.

Sleip grønske over mørke steinar
på båe sider
i dette låge vassmål.
Døden i båten er tagal.
Døden i båten er blind:
Han verar grønska og tek i steinane,
tek i steinar og slepper,
glid på sitt sund
fram og attende,
fomlar etter plassen for eit garn.

Båten er styrd av ain blind
og garnet kjem ut som det fell seg.
Det rundar seg litt, som i vind,
men berre eit kast imot ingen,
ein leik med sin ynde før arbeid.

Båten kjem bort att, ved ukjende hamrar,
fortast råd under ukjende hamrar
—og sakte sig garnet i sundet.

Fishing Grounds

In dusk and drizzle
the net sinks down in the cove,
stretches over the sound,
buries itself in the silt
and hides on the bottom.
The boat slides quietly along
and the helmsman is silent,
the figure at the helm is still.

Slimy green on black rocks
surrounds the shoals
and death in the boat is quick
and death in the boat is blind:
he smells the green,
touches the stones
and then pulls back,
glides over the cove
looking for a place
to drop his net.

The blind-steered prow turns this way and that,
the net unfurls aimlessly
billows in the whims of wind,
a random cast,
a bit of graceful play before the work.

The skiff turns toward unfamiliar cliffs
and the net sinks slowly, softly into the wake

Sakte sig maskene
rute for rute
fine og løynde
mot botnens stein,
mot botnens slam og svevn,
mot botnens store samling.
Kjempetre ligg der
sidan tusen år,
slamrygger er det,
garnet spenner rutene,
ordnar seg vidare,
strekker seg, bratnar og står.
Ovanfrå mørknar det.
Nedanfrå stilnar det.
Så er det ferdig uti Garnsund.

mesh upon mesh
melting together
toward the rocks of the bottom,
toward the sludge and sleep of the bottom,
toward the harvest of the bottom.
Titan trees lying there,
for a thousand years, reposed—
mudridges now.
The net flexes its muscles,
constricts, then stretches,
grows taut
stands still.
Above it, darkness grows.
Below, silence flows. Thus
all is finished in the cove.

Alltid lenger

Trådane frå vårt indre
vil alltid lenger,
fomlande etter eitt: det inste.

Inste eld.
Inste kjelde.

Aldri vil vi få det,
vi tolde ikkje ha det,
endå går vi søker,
drøymer om det, vaker,
hyller dei som borar
i einsemd fram på leia,
ein for ein i mørkret
—mørkt dei vil ha sundsprengt
for sitt liv!

Dirren i di hand—
dirren hjå den einsame
nær ukjent.

Always Further

The threads of our inner selves
keep probing deeper, innermore
—towards the innermost:

The ultimate fountain.
The ultimate fire.

Never grasping, nor could we
bear to hold it, still
we grope, dream
and waking, envy
those who reach the deepest loneliness,
the darkness
forfeiting life
to crush the dark.

Your hand trembles—
so, too, the lonely,
when he meets the unknown.

Forbrenninga

Vi vik attende:
alt mørkt logar opp der
før det når botn.

Stille draging til deg
krater, i vår draum.
Men i neste stund har vi sansa,
stenger, vik frå og går bort.
Vi vil ikkje ha oppbrende hagar.

Det ljuvaste finst berre eingong.
Frukt daskar mot frukt i vår li,
seier vi sakte og vakkert
der vi har våre ljuvaste stunder—
Og det ljuvaste er berre eingong.

Krateret,
der mørke flak losnar på veggen
i innmura kvelv
og stuper mot det kvitglødande,
reinbrent i ein useieleg sekund—
vi rys attende for det,

men samstundes losnar det i oss
stille, *mot* forbrenning
just some stundene i liene
er på sitt høgste.

Burning

We drift back:
where everything burns
before it reaches bottom.

Gently drawn to you,
crater, in our dream.
Yet in that instant
we feel the flame
we draw together, shrink back
and flee.
We don't want burned gardens.

The loveliest things are only once,
fruit brushes fruit in our meadow—
we say slowly and fondly
There where we pass our loveliest times
and the best things are only once.

From the crater—
where charred cinders flake off the walls
and flutter toward the white-hot glow,
burnt clean in one purging moment—
we draw back.
Yet are drawn to burning.

Just when the times in the woods
are at their best.

Frostdagen

Kva var det
med ein gong skulle vi gå—?
Med ein gong
var det rasende frost?
Og utan vidare sette vi til sprangs
for å koma attende til sommaren,
men så kaldt var det at fotslaga let holt,
skræmande som over gravkvelvingar.
Marka var stein.
Vi skjøna det ikkje.

Nei nei vi skjøna det ikkje—
Kring føtene *våre* spratt så visst
ikkje blomane fram.

Det dunka berre holare mot tome kvelvingar
i telen.
Marka gjorde seg berre hardare og hardare
under vekta vår.
Kunne vi skjøne slikt?

Men same kva vi gjorde
så dunka det taktfast i telen,
og vi sprang utan opphald
for å koma inn i sommaren,
men det var tørr frost alle stader,
sus av frost alle stader,

Frosty Day

Why did we have to go just then?
Just when the frost came thick
and sudden
and we turned to run
to return to summer.
But in that cold our steps rang hollow
as on the tops of tombs.
Ground like granite
we could not understand.

How could we understand it
around our feet
nothing bloomed.

The ground only sounded more hollow
over the empty earth
and grew harder under our weight—
How could we understand?
Our steps pounded down on the frozen land
and we ran
to reach the summer
—everywhere

ingen verdens ting såg vi anna enn
skjerande frost.

Då sa det: din liljefot—
Då sa det: din fine draum—
Då sa det: tida er ute.

the chewing frost
the biting chill
the gnawing cold

Then it said: Your lilyfoot
Then it said: Your lovely dream—
Then it said: The time is up.

Nattvakt

Den store pendelen
er over huset.
Den vesle messingpendelen
svingar på veggen inne.
Og det gamle trøytte hjarta i kråa
pendlar på det siste
under vår vakt.

Skugge over andleta.
Skugge over klokka
—tre er ho blive—
alt er tunnsliti.
Pendelen glimtar
alt er tunnsliti.
Store pendelen
står i hogg.

Andlet er tunne
oppatt og oppatt
andlet er tunne
store pendelen
store pendel
i hogg—

der, inni dødsstilla, talar
ho som har brukt opp sine stunder
og no blir vakt ved i natta,
og alt heng tunt som i tråd.

Nightwatch

The giant pendulum
hangs over the house.
The small brass pendulum
swings on the wall
inside
and the haggard heart in bed
beats its last
under our watchful eye.

Shadow on the face,
shadow on the clock
—it's three now—
everything is running down.

The pendulum shimmers
all is run down.
The big pendulum poises,
ready to fall.

The faces are thin
again and again
faces are thin
the big pendulum
big pendulum
—falls—

there is deathly quiet, the one
speaks who has used up her time

Ho som i dyktige hender
samla kvar streng i huset,
spør no i småe timar
sakte om hjelp og råd.
————og når han så høgg,
utpå dagsida,
lyner han over land og hav
over mo og avgrunn,
og finn deg, flydd og bortgøymd
og forklædd
i di ungdoms li,
silande av overskot som eingong.

and is now watched over in the night
and on a thread everything hangs.

She whose helping hands
held every thread in that house
now asks in the early hours
for comfort and counsel.

————and when he then strikes
toward dawn,
he flashes across sea and land
over cliff and moor
and finds you, far off
secluded, disguised
in the woods of your youth,
oozing with energy, as before.

Skuggane på neset

Svarte skuggar sig om nes utan opphald
og utan ljod,
for slik er det i vår hug.

Slik samlast vi på neset
etter som dagen minkar.
Og etter som ljoset minkar
står vi alt stillare,
utan å fortelje grunnen.
Stillare og stillare
på våre nes.
Det vart ein heit dag
å koma igjennom,
kunne vi sagt.
Ein logande dag.
Men vi teier.

Vi kjenner berre dagen som ein slokna klang.
No kjenner vi kvelden, lang og forunderleg.
Varme steinar etter brennande sol
som no er borte.
Dirrande aningar og sjølvlysande minne.
Nedtrakka blomar og knuste bilete,
og såre kne.
Alt det vi ikkje ville gjort
gjorde vi sju gonger.
Så var det slutt.

Shadows on the Headland

Inky shadows sink down on the headland
where gathering silence stands
as too in our mind.

So we gather on the headland
as the day grows frail,
the light more pale
and we stand quieter,
quieter, without giving reasons,
on our headlands.

It was a hot day
to get through—
we could have said,
a burning hot day
but we keep quiet.

We remember the day as an extinguished sound;
now we feel the chill of evening, long and awesome
—warm stones after fevered sun,
now gone.
Glimmering premonitions, shining memories,
trampled blossoms, broken pictures
and sore knees. All
we would not have done
and did, seven times.
Then it was over.

Men her på neset kan vi ikkje vera
for det—
Vi står her berre, ventar noko nytt.
Ved alle brende nes glid elvar,
og på neset står skuggane og blygest,
og ventar båten.
Den årelause båten er vår lodd.
All styring teken frå oss.

Vi står her i di djupe natt, Natt,
og ventar det nye bak odden.
Straumen går svart og stille.
Og det vi kjenner ved det
fortel vi ikkje til einannen.

But here on the headland
we cannot stay,
we only stand, delay
and wait for something new.
Beyond all burnt headlands, rivers flow
and on the headland growing shadows stand
and wait for the boat;
the boat without oars
is our fate.
Rudderless.

We stand here in your darkness, Night,
await the New beyond the headland,
the current grows black and still.
And what we know of this
we do not tell each other.

Tomse-legende

Det ropte til den tomsemann
det gode rop i tomsars land:
No er det nok, kom over!
Det kalla i hans ringe bol
frå bortom måne stjerner sol:
no er det nok, kom over!

Og tomsen ned til stranda gjekk.
Ein liten flir i lufta hekk:
Han trur det ropar over—
Men straks han rørde mørke flod
så skilde vatnet seg og stod
—så gjekk han hastig over.

Fool's Legend

The fool was summoned by the call,
the call of never-never:
it is enough, come over!
It called him from his little house
from far beyond the moon and stars:
it is enough, come over!

And the fool went down to the river's edge
bathed in smiles of scorn,
he believed he was called over—
But just as he reached the river's edge
the waters parted—stood still
and then he walked hurriedly over.

Som ein drøymande hund?

Er du hunden?
Hundlekket gnagar ovnsfoten under draum,
og utstrekt på teppet ligg dyret uskuldig,
uskuldig og blundar
—men jaktdraumen går
med kvink og brårykk.
Markene er sæle og blodige.

Er du hunden?
Det står ingen over *deg*
og finn deg ut.
Den fælslege løyndomen
får du ha i fred.

Men du er vel hunden.
Dine rå jaktmarker,
med blodstriper i morgonrimet,
og hendingar som aldri blir
fortalde som dei var:
om skamsprengt liv
som gøymer seg i busken
og blir attfunni av deg.
Av deg—
Om kjelder
som dei mødde ville drikke i
og møtte deg i staden.
—Og din hundedraum varer

Letting Dreaming Dogs Lie

What have you to do
with dreaming dogs,
sprawled on rugs, innocently lying
—eyes twitching in jerks and spasms—
chasing unseen game over phantom ground,
whose leash is chafing
the leg of the stove?
The dreamhunt goes on
over happy yet bloody ground.

What has this dog to do
with you?
You have no master
to find you out,
to learn the sordid secret
you withhold.

But perhaps you are the dog—
Your hunting grounds are bloody with tracks in the
                    morning dew
and episodes never told as they really were:
about dead-tired life, found cringing in bushes,
hunted, hounded to death—
by you.
About gleaming streams
where the weary long to drink
and are trapped instead

bak attletne augelok,
og jarnlekket held alt innom grensa
som i ein kvævande ring,
så det gnissar i malmfoten
alt er fest i. I dei lange
lange nettene når ingen held vakt.
Sleppe det laus får du ikkje.
Nokon du ikkje kjenner, har trass alt bundi deg
før fallet.
Koma deg bort innom ringen
kan du ikkje. Innanfor det stutte lekket
har du å velje:
har du å fri deg der du er,
og utan vitne, skilje det ut av deg,
eller tærast opp.

by you.
Your dogdream lasts
behind closed eyelids
and the chain holds fast
within that strangling ring,
grates on the iron leg
on which everything is based
in the endless nights
when nobody wakes.
You cannot escape—
some master has leashed you
you cannot slip away;
within your tiny circle
you must choose:
to free yourself
by waking, or dozing
be consumed.

Hete

Dei kjære aldri nemner det.
Men andre seier: her stod eg,
det var ein fredag,
og akkurat her—

Kring heile grannelaget femner det:
Minnest det var fredag,
minnest etter frostnetter
minnest etter tele,
marka hard over indre ukjent
—i dette kunne det koma
utan varsel, og det kom:
Utan vidare revna her i underlege mønster
braut fram glødande sidan lange tider,
skok dei støaste, sette i brann ikring seg,
slutta ikkje før alt var uttømt,
øydde seg sjølv, og mørkna
—var ikkje jordlag og tele,
var ein venleg daglegdags mann.

Heat

The loving speak not of it
while others say: on a Friday, here—
on this spot—
I stood—
Exactly here.

And through the neighborhood, they spread the news:
remember that day, a Friday?
remember, before the thaw?
remember, after the bitter cold nights?
and the ground frozen hard over buried secrets?
—and here, without a word of warning,
it could come
and came: Just like that
the earth swelled and cracked
it glowed from within
and then
erupted
shaking all that had been
so solid, firm,
till all was overturned, then
turned back upon itself again
and darkened
—and was neither earth nor frost
but warmth and flesh.

Hans kjære var hans kjære til han brann.
Grannelaget kjende han:
Hans ro. Hans enkle tale.
Hans tagalle strenge liv
med veike gøymde søkk i, kjende få.
Nettene var hans eigne, og unemnde av soga.

Slagghaugar i lendet:
Halvgløymde utbrot.
Livlause rester
og samstundes minning
om dei løynde eldanes land.
Her er det meste bak skalet,
her må det koma som utbrot,
her må dei tære seg sjølve
med underjords hete og vald.

Men varsel fekk dei, om det store, dei han drogst til.
No etterpå skjønar dei det var fullbyrding, alt.
Auga hans lengta mot fullbyrding—
veit dei no.
Dei *venta* det frigjorde ropet frå han,
og var sjølve ferdige å møte
—slik og han visste *det*
og hadde sine motrop klar
—slik farleg vekselspel blir planlagt.
Og når skuggen er større enn slagghaugar,
        revnar det.

Whose loved ones loved him
till he burned.
His neighbors knew him, too:
His quiet way. His simple speech.
Although his inner life, few knew:
The lonely nights that were his own
and his alone, were only known
to him.

Heaps of cinder all around—
eruptions half-forgotten.
Dead refuse.
And the dim remembrance
of another time, another place
—the land of hidden fires.
Hidden under heavy crust
waiting for eruption,
and the heat of the netherworld
—fires that feed upon themselves.

But those he chose were forewarned
and afterwards they knew
that all was fulfilled.
All his eye had longed for,
knew they then.
They awaited the sign,
knew his freeing word would come,
were ready to respond
as he had planned
—the risky game was played.
And when the shadows lengthen on the cinderheaps
it begins.

Når vona om løysing er lengst borte, revnar det.
Ein frostmorgon revna det ikringom,
og alt innom synsvidd vart vitne
med elden frå under kom naken.

Lufta vart næring, rasande næring,
sugande nedi
og inn.
Revnene kom undantil,
rann bortover som ormar,
auka seg og sprengde
—midt i det kom grunn-duren,
opna sine sluser,
så kvar som stod her høyrde
stod klumsa i sitt indre,
kvar som var vitne, kjende skuld.

Han brann, og ropte i sin vande, si frigjering.
Revnene vart gap. Sundsprengde frostkantar.
Fullt fullt av frigjort!
Elden som lufta trekte sugande ned mot,
røyk som dreiv bort då logen vart heitare,
så allting låg opent som det *er*
mellom menneske.
Han ropte sine rop i lette,

With hope of deliverance long-since gone
it begins.
One chill morning, it breaks through all around
and everything
as far as the eye can see
is witness to the fire
that flames naked from below.

The air was wedded to the flames,
drawn down
and in
to feed the hungry fire.
The cracks which came from deep within
ran along the ground like writhing snakes,
quickly grew to quakes
that tore earth apart.
—Then the thunder of the earth
stunned all who heard
and all who heard felt guilt.

He burned,
crying in relief and pain.
Crevices grew to gorges,
parting the edges of frost.
A warm breath of freedom
the air drew to the flames
smoke drifted away
so that all was exposed, laid open to the core
between people.
His cries were relief

om det som hadde brunni
utan luft.
Underleg var det, hjelpelaust og vågsamt:
Rop som ingen forstod mellom braka,
andres uskjønlege svar attende,
og som hans eigne førebudde mot-rop slo i svime,
ord som ingen ville skjøna, om det så var stilt.

Tett tett innpå var dei kjære,
for å mildne, for å stenge,
bli herre over utbrotet
—i røynsle etter småutbrot frå før.
Men dette skok frå djupare enn der dei var,
frå der ingen kan skjøne eller mildne.
Sjå fekk dei og at han ikkje prøvde sløkke,
såg at han ville det, det løyste dei frå redsla,
det er vi! ropte dei endå, til fånyttes i larmen,
og mot glødande floder av underjord.
Til fånyttes i larmen,
men dei såg dei var hans eigne
heile tida, der krateret brann reint.
—Medan andre, som også var støkt no og trong
              fred:
venlege han hadde vendt seg til,
fått hjelp av i sin veikskap,
brått utakksamt lagdest øyde, vart trekt inni
og strauk med.
Det er vi! sa og slike, hemmelege, hjelparar,
i all sin rett,
men retten forkomst,
ingen såg dei,
deira små hus sveid av.

for that which had burned within
until now
without air.
Wondrous, so frail yet fearless:
the cries none heard above the thundercrash,
and the answers echoing back
which none would hear
even if all were
quiet.

Close by were the loving
to close the wounds, to soothe the shocks
—forewarned by lesser tremors.
But this had shaken from depths
too deep to soothe
and when they saw that he longed to soothe it
but would not try
their fear subsided.
We are with you, they called,
all in vain in the roar and
in the fiery rivers of the netherworld,
for when they saw the crater burned clean
they saw they had always been his.
—while other friendly ones he'd turned to,
took comfort in his seeming weakness,
who desired peace as well,
and were in that moment turned to ash.
We are with you, also said those furtive allies
who thought the right too pure, too precious to lose,
rich with righteousness never used
saw their fragile shelters burn.

Han stod der og fylte sine tunge ord,
uskjønlege ord, og brann.
Å, stive mørke novemberring av vitne:
slik er elden.
Natt vart det ikkje om dagen lakka,
det lyste frå lånte kjelder
så lenge dette mennesket varde.
Vara altfor lenge slapp det i si fullbyrdingstrå:
Ropinga av viktige bodskap vart dauvare,
duren i grunnen veikna og vart borte
og heten svalna seg i vinden.
Hans kjære stod fast på sine postar,
kjende seg ikkje knuste, men lyfte
—der eldberget kjøltest og stilna,
mørkna i fred til ein slagghaug.

He bled there, oozed precious words
unheard—
and burned.
In the dark November's night:
such is the fire. The light,
still glowing when his day had died,
shone from borrowed sources,
as long as his flesh would last.
Which was not long
the words soon faded,
the thunder grew faint
the light failed
and died away
and the heat cooled in a rising wind.
His chosen ones stood fast
and waited,
not crushed, but elated
—while the mountain of fire
cooled and silent at last
turned peacefully into a mound of ash.

Fuglen av logen

Opp av den herja grunnen
vil det stige
nytt, men kjenneleg og ukueleg,
det du er i pakt med.

Kor lenge har du kalla i fåfengd?
Ikkje eit sekund.
Til fåfengd kallar ingen i mørke netter,
det er berre du som ikkje ser.

Du græt over det øydde
og strøyer oske på deg sjølv
og ser ikkje Fuglen Føniks
inni logen.

Kallar du
kallar du enno?

The Bird in the Flame

From devastated earth
new forms will rise
but what at first offends our eyes
will at last be seen as welcome birth.

How long did we cry vainly
in the long and endless nights?
Not even seconds.
In the dark, no one cries in vain—
we only fail to see.

We bewail the ruin in our view
and strew ourselves with ashes
and do not see the Phoenix
in the flames.

Do you still cry?
Do you still cry out?

Appendix

Tarjei Vesaas in English Translation

Novels

The Birds (Fuglane, 1957). Translated by Torbjørn Støverud and Michael Barnes. London: Peter Owen, 1968; New York: William Morrow & Co., 1969.

The Boat in the Evening (Båten om kvelden, 1968). Translated by Elizabeth Rokkan. London: Peter Owen, 1971.

The Bridges (Bruene, 1966). Translated by Elizabeth Rokkan. London: Peter Owen, 1969.

The Great Cycle (Det store spelet, 1934). Translated by Elizabeth Rokkan, with an Introduction by Harald S. Næss. Madison: University of Wisconsin Press, 1967.

The Ice Palace (Is-slottet, 1963). Translated by Elizabeth Rokkan. London: Peter Owen, 1966.

The Seed (Kimen, 1940) and *Spring Night (Vårnatt,* 1954). Translated by Kenneth G. Chapman. New York: American Scandinavian Foundation; Oslo: Universitetsforlaget, 1964.

Short Stories

"In the Fish's Golden Youth" ("I fiskens grønne ungdom," from *Ein vakker dag,* 1959). Translated by Tim Schiff. *American-Scandinavian Review,* 56, no. 3 (1968), 287-90.

"Never Tell It" ("Aldri fortelje det," from *Leiret og hjulet,* 1936). Translated by Kenneth G. Chapman. *American-Scandinavian Review,* 47, no. 2 (1959), 166-71.

"Snow" (Det snør og snør," from *Ein vakker dag,* 1959). Translated by Kenneth G. Chapman. *Literary Review,* 12, no. 2 (1969), 170-75.

"Twenty-one" ("21 år," from *Leiret og hjulet,* 1936). Translated by Kenneth G. Chapman. In *New World Writing,* no 14, pp. 269-80. New York: New American Library, 1958.

Poems

"In Deep Liability" ("I ansvars naud," from *Leiken og lynet,* 1947).

Translated by Robert Bly. *Literary Review*, (Teaneck, N.J.) 12, no. 2 (1969), 222.

"Once upon a Time" ("Det var eingong . . . ," from *Leiken og lynet*, 1947). Translated by Martin and Inga Allwood. In *Twentieth Century Scandinavian Poetry*, pp. 171-72. Oslo: Gyldendal, 1950.

"One Rows and Rows" ("Det ror og ror," from *Lykka for ferdesmenn*, 1949). Translated by James W. Brown. *Literary Review* (Teaneck, N.J.), 12, no. 2, 218-19.

"Rain in Hiroshima" ("Regn i Hiroshima," from *Leiken og lynet*, 1947). Translated by James W. Brown. *Literary Review* (Teaneck, N.J.), 12, no. 2, 220-21.

"Rain in Hiroshima" *(Regn i Hiroshima,"* from *Leiken og lynet*, 1947). Translated by Fritz H. König. *Micromegas* (Amherst, Mass.), 4, no. 3 (1971), 28.

"Snow and Fir Forests" ("Snø og granskog," from *Kjeldene*, 1946). Translated by Martin and Inga Allwood. *Twentieth Century Scandinavian Poetry*, pp. 170-71. Oslo: Gyldendal, 1950.

Tarjei Vesaas: 30 Poems. Selected, translated, and with an introduction by Kenneth G. Chapman. Oslo: Universitetsforlaget, 1964.

Born in 1897 on the ancient Vesaas farmstead in Vinje district, Telemark, Tarjei Vesaas published the first of his many novels drawn from rural Norwegian life in 1923. His last appeared in 1968, two years before his death.

Vesaas turned to poetry in his latter years, his first collection appearing in 1946. *Land of Hidden Fires (Løynde eldars land)* was published in 1953. At the time of his death in 1970, Vesaas was recognized as a key figure in Norwegian and Scandinavian literature.

Fritz König is assistant professor of German and Norwegian at the University of Northern Iowa. Co-translator Jerry Crisp is assistant professor of English at the same university.

The book was designed by Helene Skora. The typeface for the text is Caledonia designed by W. A. Dwiggins; and the display face is Optima.

The text is printed on Neutratext paper and the book is bound in Columbia Mills' Fictionette Natural Finish cloth over binders' boards. Manufactured in the United States of America.

125